DIADEM

Look for the other books in the

Book of Earth

John Peel

AN
APPLE
PAPERBACK

SCHOLASTIC INC.
New York Toronto London Auckland Sydney

Cover art by Jean Pierre Targete

No part of this publication may be reproduced in whole or in part, or stored in a retrieval system, or transmitted in any form or by any means, electronic, mechanical, photocopying, recording, or otherwise, without written permission of the publisher. For information regarding permission, write to Scholastic Inc., Attention: Permissions Department, 555 Broadway, New York, NY 10012.

ISBN 0-590-14965-2

12 11 10 9 8 7 6 5 4 3 2 1   8 9/9 0 1 2 3/0

Printed in the U.S.A.   40
First Scholastic printing, February 1998

For Craig Walker

PROLOGUE

"He must come to Earth," Toshiro said, looking down at the girl in the wheelchair. "Everything has been set in motion. The trap has been laid."

The young girl nodded. It seemed almost to exhaust her. "Score is my only hope," she said softly. "My only chance to be freed from this prison. But will all three of them come? The amulet can only compel Score."

The Japanese man moved to stare out the window. "We have used what meager powers we have," he replied. "I have managed to see something of what has happened on other worlds. We know Score has bonded with two friends, Helaine and Pixel. I do not think it likely that they will abandon their friend. Quite the contrary, I am almost certain that they will insist on accompanying him to Earth."

"And then?" the girl prompted. She sounded hopeful at last.

"Then our . . . business associate, Mr. Caruso, will find them for us," Toshiro replied.

The girl shifted uncomfortably. "We seem to be placing a great deal of reliance on this man," she observed softly. She gestured at a computer on the desk beside her. "I have done some checking up on him. He is generally known as 'Bad Tony,' and was in jail until a few days ago. Can he be trusted?"

"No," Toshiro answered honestly. "He has admitted that he has a reason of his own for wanting Score. He is, after all, the boy's father. But while he cannot be trusted, he is predictable. He will not betray us, because we have the power to return him to the custody of the police. He barely escaped from the jail that held him the first time. A second attempt is not likely to be successful. He has a great fear of confinement, and this makes him controllable. Knowing the weakness of an enemy gives you power over him; knowing the weakness of an ally makes him unlikely to desert you."

Toshiro inclined his head slightly. "Mr. Caruso can be managed, and his men will capture the trio when they return to Earth. Very shortly, they will be in my hands." He turned back to the girl. "And then Score will have to help free you from your current state."

The girl slapped her hands down on her unfeeling legs. "He *must* help me!" she cried. "I cannot endure much more of this waiting!"

"They will help you," promised Toshiro. "I will see to it. Score will help you — or else face my wrath."

CHAPTER 1

When Score awoke, it was to an immediate surge of pain. He gasped and struggled to sit upright.

"Take it easy," Helaine said to him. The concern in her voice surprised Score. "You've had a rough experience."

"You're telling me?" Score asked. His chest ached. "I feel like someone tried to rip my heart out." He looked around the small bedroom in the castle he'd adopted for himself. Pixel and Oracle were also there. Both looked as worried as Helaine sounded. "What happened to me?"

"You collapsed in pain," Pixel said. "We brought you here so you could recover." He glanced at the black-clad man beside him. "Uh, Oracle has some bad news."

Score tried to recover some of his normal humor. "When has he ever brought us *good* news?" he asked. Then he looked at the messenger. He wasn't actually real, in the normal sense of the word. He was a projection of some kind who had once served the Triad. Now he was free, and he had decided to help the three of them. Whenever he showed up, though, it always spelled trouble. "So what's the bad word this time? I'll never be able to play the violin again?"

"It's worse than that, I'm afraid," Oracle replied. "You are not likely to get better in the immediate future. Quite the contrary, in fact. You are in serious trouble."

This would have depressed Score, except he could hardly get more depressed than he was right now. He could remember fainting because of the agony that had torn through his body. The idea that it could get worse made him sick. "So what's wrong with me? A bad heart or something? Incurable cancer?"

Oracle shook his head. "No, it is nothing medical. It is a magical attack, and it is just beginning."

Score sighed, and lay back on his bed. "Oy. *Another* mad magician?"

"No," Oracle replied. "This is actually low-level

magic. Very primitive. And unfortunately, very effective."

Helaine glared at him. "Can you stop being cryptic for a minute and actually *explain* what you're talking about?" she demanded.

"I'll try. I'm sure you recall that when you went up against Sarman, he used dolls to control you. To animate those dolls, he needed your shape, form, and substance. Once he had those, you were forced to do whatever he commanded."

Pixel caught on. "So you're saying that someone, somewhere has made a doll of Score and is using it against him."

"Not a doll, no," Oracle answered. "This is very primitive magic. What they're doing is using something very personal that belonged to Score, and they've put a wasting spell on it. This spell will attack him through the object they have, causing cumulative harm. It will attack progressively until it kills Score."

"Two questions," Score broke in, before his friends could start. "First, *what* does this person have of mine? Second, how do I stop them?"

Oracle shrugged. "What they have I cannot say. Only that it isn't something simple like your old clothes. It must be something intimately connected with you. Something that means a lot to you."

Score snorted. "There's very little this important to me," he stated. "So what about question two?"

"That's easier and harder to answer," Oracle admitted.

"Marvelous," Score complained. "Trust you not to have a straightforward answer for me."

"It's easy in the sense that you must track down the object and recover it," Oracle explained. "It's harder because I do not know what it is, where it is, who has it, or why they are doing this to you. You will need to know all of that before you can recover."

"Then it sounds as if we're going to have to get busy," Helaine said practically.

"At least we have a good idea of where to start," added Pixel. "The only place Score could really have left anything that's valuable to him is back on Earth. We've been with him pretty constantly ever since, and we'd have noticed if he'd left anything valuable anywhere on the way."

"When I left Earth, I didn't exactly have a lot of possessions," Score told his friends. "My mother died when I was six, and the less I saw of my father, the happier I was. He never gave me presents, and I never gave him anything."

"There must nevertheless be something there that is of great value to you in some way," insisted Oracle. "Perhaps you will discover what it is soon."

"And that means a trip to see Shanara," Pixel decided. "She's our best bet here. If anyone can help us again, she can."

Score realized that Pixel was correct. Shanara was another magic-user, who lived on a world called Rawn. She wasn't as powerful as the three of them, but she had some very strong specialized magic. She was also far more experienced than they were, having practiced her magic for at least ten years longer than they had. She specialized in magic that could disguise her true appearance, enabling her to become any kind of living creature she desired. Score thought this was something of a waste because in her normal form she was a very beautiful woman.

It was another of her abilities that they needed now. Shanara excelled in discovering information. She had a magic pool of water that she used to see other worlds and peoples. She called this sight *scrying*. Using this, she might be able to locate what was being used against Score.

Helaine nodded, obviously having reached the same conclusion. She looked down at Score. "You must stay here and rest," she said. "Pixel and I will go and see if she can help us."

"Forget it, bossy," Score answered. "I'm the one who's being attacked. And if Oracle is right, the attacks are only going to get worse. I'm not staying here, waiting to die. I'm coming with you. In between attacks, I'm perfectly all right." This was actually a lie; he did, in fact, feel terrible. But he simply *couldn't* just lie there, hoping his friends would save his life.

"You're being impractical and stubborn," Helaine complained.

"Yes, and I know they're usually your fields of expertise," Score joked, "but for this once, I'm practicing them, too." He managed to sit up. "Anyway, it looks like the trail leads to Earth, and you'd be totally lost there. It's my home, so you'll need me to help you survive. Besides, I could really go for a slice of pizza."

Pixel gently placed his hand on Score's shoulder. "You don't fool me," he said. "You're not in as good shape as you pretend." Then he shook his head. "Unfortunately, you're also right that we would need you on Earth, if that is where the trail leads us. So I agree that you'd be better off coming with us."

Helaine scowled. "You're on his side?" she grumbled. "I think he should stay here and conserve his strength."

"Even if the suspense kills me?" complained Score. "No way." He took a deep breath and managed to stand up. The room stopped swaying after about twenty seconds. "I can manage. And I want to find out who's doing this to me. Then I'll rip *their* heart out of their chest with my bare fingers and see how they like it."

Shaking her head, Helaine said, "Well, I seem to be outvoted. You're coming along, then. But I still think you're being very foolish."

Score managed a weak grin. "Hey, you want me to stop a habit of a lifetime now?" He put a hand on her arm. "I know you're only thinking of what's best for me," he added seriously. "Trust me, going with you is a lot better than waiting here. I couldn't stand that. Put yourself in my position: If this were you being attacked, would you let Pixel and me go off without you?"

Helaine smiled slightly. "You'd never make it without me," she replied. "All right, you've made your point. But I don't want you to complain later that you made the wrong decision."

"Cross my heart," Score promised. "If I have one left after the next attack." He turned to Oracle. "How long will that be?"

Oracle shrugged. "I cannot say. This was the second attack, and it came eight hours after your first. Perhaps it will be another eight hours before the next, or perhaps it will be less. It is possible that the attacks will come closer together as they go on."

"Well, you're a real ray of sunshine," grumbled

Score. He turned back to Helaine and Pixel. "Then it sounds like the less time we waste, the better. We should head for Shanara's palace as soon as possible. You know, once upon a time, I thought that magic could solve any problems. But the more we learn, the less confident I feel. And the less safe." He grimaced. "Not that I've ever felt safe since my mother died." Even though it had been years before, the memory of this brought a lump to his throat. His mother had been the only person in his life Score had ever loved or trusted. Until, maybe, Helaine and Pixel. And Thunder, the leader of the unicorn herd he had befriended. He couldn't remember much about his mother, except an impression of dark hair, a radiant smile, and a vague memory of a locket.

A locket. . . .

Of course.

Score slapped his forehead. "Boy, am I ever dumb!"

"Well, you won't get any argument from me about that," Helaine promised him.

"I've just realized what it could be that we're looking for," Score explained. "I was thinking about my mother, and how I don't remember much about her. But I do remember a locket she used to wear. She would sing me to sleep at night, and I would see that locket swaying back and forth over my face. She had a lock of my baby hair in it from the first time I ever had a haircut."

"That could be it!" agreed Oracle, excitedly. "Do you have any idea where it is?"

"Well, I know where it isn't," Score answered. "Shortly before I came onto the circuit of the Diadem, I went back to my old apartment. The only thing I found was a letter my mother had hidden there. There was no sign of the locket. I guess my father must have taken it."

"So we look for your father then?" asked Pixel.

Helaine said sympathetically, "I know how your father mistreated you. This can't be easy for you, having to face him again."

"Face him?" Score shook his head. "We can't do that. He's in prison. Which means he can't possibly have the locket. It's got to be somewhere else, and I don't have a clue where." To be honest, he was glad that he wouldn't have to deal with Bad Tony again. He'd lived in terror of his father for as long as he could remember. He'd endured cruel words and crueler beatings, and he still shivered at the thought of ever having to meet him again.

That was about the only thing to be glad of right now: that whatever happened on Earth, he wouldn't have to face his father again.

CHAPTER 2

Helaine was worried. Though Score was talking and acting bravely — which was unusual enough for him — she could tell he was nowhere near as strong as he claimed to be. His skin was pale, his veins showing slightly beneath the skin. His eyes were dark-ringed, and his body moved slowly. If she had any choice in the matter, she'd have insisted that he stay behind. But she'd been outvoted, and she'd have to live with it.

She only hoped that *Score* could live with it. Even though he had the right to come along, a journey to Earth was going to tax his strength severely. And if there was any trouble, he might even prove to be a liability.

There was a tightness in Helaine's throat as she realized that she had grown to be very fond of Score. If anything happened to him, it would really hurt her. This surprised her because she'd never been really close to anyone her own age before. Growing up in her father's castle she'd been the daughter of Lord Votrin, and therefore far too good for anyone to associate with. Or else, in her disguise as the boy Renald, she'd been too lowly for anyone to bother with. Her father had been very distant and aloof, completely uninterested in her except as a convenient bargaining tool — aiming to marry her off to cement an alliance. Her only true friend had been her father's old war trainer, who had kept her secret and taught her to fight.

And now she'd allowed herself to get friendly with both Score and Pixel. They, at least, treated her as an equal, though this hadn't been very easy at first for Score. She couldn't lose one of her few friends now.

She prepared herself for the Portal casting. To travel across the worlds of the Diadem, Portals were necessary. They could only be formed by magic-users of some strength, and they opened a rift in space between two worlds. The Diadem was formed in a number of circuits, and travel had to take place between two adjacent worlds. Since their current location on

Dondar was on the Inner Circuit, there was no direct access to Earth, an Outer World. They had to cross first to the Middle Circuit world of Rawn, and then on to the Outer Circuit world of Treen. This was where Shanara had her home, in the mountains above the planet's goblin kingdom.

Helaine opened her Book of Magic, and found the correct spell. She and Pixel then joined their strengths together and formed the Portal. A jagged deep blackness formed in the air in front of the three of them. Helaine briefly wished that she had taken the time to say good-bye to her unicorn friend, Flame, but this was an emergency, with no time for nonessentials. She gestured for Score to go through the Portal first, in case he stumbled, and then she followed. When Pixel came through the Portal vanished, leaving them on Rawn.

A cold wind whipped into them, and Helaine shivered. She'd forgotten just how chilly it could get on the top of the mountain. Luckily, it was a fairly nice day, with no more than two feet of snow and ice to wade through as they struggled against the bitter wind, heading for the shimmering castle about a quarter of a mile away. It shone in the cold sunlight, looking as if it had been formed from ice itself.

The three of them staggered on, Helaine and Pixel both watching Score intently in case he needed help. He was clearly aware that they were watching him, and he pressed on, refusing to acknowledge that he might be in trouble. Although Helaine almost admired his stubbornness, she hoped he wouldn't take it too far.

When they reached the courtyard, the gate was open, and they stumbled inside. Here they were shielded from the stinging wind, which made them feel a great deal better. The three of them hurried into the main building. Despite the veneer of iciness, this was made of good, solid stone, covered with beautiful, rich tapestries that made the castle a good deal warmer than the world outside.

"You must be frozen," Shanara said as she hurried to greet them. "If you'd let me know you were coming, I'd have met you with furs. Oracle has only just arrived and told me you were on your way. Come on, come on, it's warm in my study." The lovely blonde sorceress ushered them into her room, and waved them to chairs. There were steaming mugs of deliciously scented liquid awaiting them. Helaine sipped hers with pleasure. It tasted unusual, with a hint of chocolate and malt. It warmed her almost immediately.

Oracle was standing beside one of Shanara's bookcases. There was no sign of Blink, Shanara's fuzzy red panda. He was intelligent and magical himself. He was also incredibly lazy, and was undoubtedly off somewhere taking one of his naps.

"Oracle tells me that you have to return to Earth," Shanara said, sounding quite concerned. She looked at Score. "That someone has an amulet that belonged to your mother, and is using it magically to attack you."

"Right," Score agreed. He seemed to be quite happy that the sorceress was worried about him. Helaine thought it was typical of Score to enjoy being the center of attention, even though it was because he was being attacked. "We thought that maybe you could help us out in finding the locket."

"I can do more than that," Shanara promised. "Once you get to Earth, you won't have the strength left to create a Portal to return here, because your magic there will be too weak. Blink and I will cross to Treen with you, and I'll prepare a Portal for you to return again. I'll be able to pick up your telepathic signal to open it."

"Thank you," Pixel said gratefully. "I hadn't thought about that, but you're right. It'll be a big help."

Shanara gave them all a smile. "I'm happy to help you in any way I can. After all, if it wasn't for you, the Diadem would be under the control of either Sarman or the Triad by now. We all owe you a tremendous debt of gratitude." She crossed to her scrying pool, which stood near the large fireplace. Helaine watched her with interest, hoping to learn something about the process.

The sorceress waved her hand over the still waters, murmuring a spell just under her breath that Helaine couldn't make out. Then she turned and called sharply, "Blink!"

From a pile of pillows, a furry snout poked into the air. "I'm busy," a lazy voice answered. "I'm having a lovely dream about food."

"If you don't get over here right now," Shanara ordered, "I'm going to send you a positively nasty nightmare about starving to death. Move it!"

With a long-suffering sigh, Blink staggered to his feet. The red panda shook his head sadly. "She'd do it, too," he complained. "She's so mean to me."

Helaine knew that this simply wasn't true: Shanara actually looked after Blink very well. But the panda was lazy and perpetually hungry, and Shanara used her threats to make him do some work from time to time. In fact, Helaine realized, Shanara and Blink were actually very fond of each other. This complaining was simply a part of their relationship that both of them secretly enjoyed.

Blink padded across the table and jumped into Shanara's arms. Together they gazed into the scrying pool. At first nothing seemed to happen, but Helaine could tell that Shanara was drawing magical power from Blink, using it to boost her own abilities.

A picture began to form in the pool. Helaine was fascinated, staring down at it. It showed a stretch of grass, and people moving around. They were all dressed very oddly and some were using odd mechanical devices, with two large wheels joined together somehow. The people were riding them. It looked to be very awkward.

Score, trying to act casual, leaned across and frowned. "It looks like Central Park," he said.

Helaine gestured at one of the people balanced on the wheels. "And what is that?" she asked. "It looks very dangerous."

Score gave her an incredulous look. "That's a bicycle. I wanted to get some for us, remember?"

"You expect *me* to get on one of those crazy things?" asked Helaine, astonished. "I don't see how anyone can possibly get it to balance. I'm *not* doing it."

Score managed a laugh. "The brave warrior woman," he observed. "Scared of a bicycle."

"I am *not* scared," Helaine snapped. "I'm just cautious."

"Whatever," scoffed Score. Helaine felt her cheeks burning. "We don't have time for them, anyway." He turned back to Shanara. "Can you tell where the locket is?"

"No," Shanara admitted. "It's guarded by magic. Not high-grade magic, but enough to be confusing to me. Besides, this Earth of yours is a strange place. I don't understand very much of what I see. So even if I do detect something, I might not be able to explain it so you can understand it. But I'll keep probing, and if I find out anything, I'll let you know."

"Great." Score looked relieved. "Now, there's just one more thing I need you to do." He gestured at Helaine and Pixel. "We have to get these two looking like regular New Yorkers."

Helaine scowled at him. "And what's wrong with the way I look?" she demanded.

"Personally, I think you look great," Score said hastily. "On you, chain mail looks great. But it's not exactly what the fashionable folks are wearing on Park Avenue. And they *definitely* don't carry swords."

Helaine frowned and looked down at herself. She wore knee-high boots — with a dagger hidden inside the left one — leggings, a tunic, and the chain mail covering. Her sword was strapped to her side. She couldn't understand why anyone on Earth would have a problem with this. Unless. . . . Maybe they had the same prejudice as her home world? "Women aren't allowed to carry weapons on your world?" she asked, a little hurt. She'd hoped to escape this problem.

"Not just women," Score assured her. "*Nobody* on my planet carries a sword."

"Then how do they defend themselves?" Helaine asked practically.

"They don't have to," Score explained. "We have police, who are supposed to do that."

"Ah." Helaine thought she was finally starting to understand it. "These police are your professional warrior caste, then?" She smiled. "Then I shall become one, and there will be no problem."

"They're not warriors as such," Score answered. "They enforce the laws."

"Oh." Helaine saw where she had gone wrong. "They are the local lord's men, who make certain his edicts and taxes are carried out. And I would be recognized as an outsider."

"No, that's not it, either." Score threw his hands into the air. "Look, why don't you just take it from me that you can't wear a sword, and you can't impersonate a police officer? This is my world, after all, and I know what I'm talking about."

Helaine touched the hilt of her sword sadly. "I do not like the idea of leaving it behind," she confessed. "But if I must, I must." She unbuckled her belt and laid it on the table. "Now am I acceptable?"

"Not quite." Score eyed her critically. "We have to get you some modern clothes. Shanara, can you help out?"

"Of course." The sorceress bent over her pool again. "I'll just focus in on one of the locals, and duplicate her clothing." She concentrated, and one image strolling on the grass sprang into sharp focus.

Helaine gasped as she saw the girl. She was wearing nothing but two small strips of cloth and sandals. "I am *not* dressing like that!" she exclaimed in horror. "The people of your world, Score, have no concept of modesty!"

Score grinned as he looked at the blonde girl in the pool. "Halter top and shorts? They'd look great on you." Then he blushed. "I mean, hey, you work out a lot. You've got the body for it."

"Never," Helaine said firmly. "I am a lady born, and I will not show off so much of my skin to all casual onlookers."

"Okay," grumbled Score. He gestured to another female figure passing by. "How about that one?"

Helaine studied the girl as Shanara brought her into focus. She seemed a lot more acceptable. She had on long leggings made of some sort of stiff blue material, and a white top, nearly identical to the kind of clothing Score wore. It covered less than her tunic, but a great deal more than the "halter top" had. "That is acceptable," she agreed.

"Good." Score sounded relieved. "Blue jeans and a T-shirt."

Shanara nodded, and muttered to herself again. Instantly, the required garments materialized on her table. Helaine realized that they were her size.

"Now for Pixel," Score said.

Pixel raised an eyebrow. "My clothing looks appropriate," he said.

"Yeah," agreed Score. "That's fine. I don't quite know how to tell you this, though. It's the rest of you that's the problem."

"The rest of me?" Pixel was puzzled.

Score sighed. "Look, I think you look fine, and all, but . . . well, *blue* skin is kind of rare on Earth. Actually, it's kind of nonexistent."

Pixel scowled. "Nobody on your world has blue skin?" He stared at his hands, and then at Score and Helaine. Finally, he looked at the picture in the pool. "Well, I can see that most people have pale skin like the two of you. But some have dark skin." He looked at Score again. "But not blue?"

"Not blue," Score said firmly. "For this trip, you're going to need a disguise."

"Not a problem," Shanara assured him. "I can cast a simple spell that will make his skin as pale as yours. It should hold up even on Earth, where the magic is weaker."

"Great," Score said. "Then let's get to it, folks." He turned to Helaine. "You'd better find another room to change in."

"I wasn't intending to do it in public," she replied, sniffing. "Though I'm sure that's probably common on your barbaric planet."

"Only on beaches," he answered.

"Ah." Helaine could understand this. "A ritualistic area, involved in worship."

"Something like that," Score agreed, chuckling. "Sun worship, in fact."

"A primitive religion," Helaine informed him. "I might have known." She left the room and found a small chamber where she could change. She removed her normal clothing with a sigh. She'd miss being properly dressed. The T-shirt was simple enough to put on, though she felt terribly vulnerable in it. It offered no protection from attack. The blue jeans, however, were another matter. They were a lot tighter than her leggings, and a lot stiffer. They would be uncomfortable to walk in. And they didn't seem to have any way of closing. Nothing to tie them into place. There was a button, which closed well, but there was an odd gap left open. It was lined with small metallic teeth, with something like a small tongue hanging down.

It took her about five minutes, but she discovered that if she pulled up the tongue, somehow the teeth meshed together and closed the gap. This puzzled and amused her. Score had mentioned that his world was more advanced than her own — though not as far as Pixel's world was — but this was the first evidence she'd seen that he was telling the truth. This teeth and tongue apparatus was quite fascinating.

When Helaine returned to the study, she stopped in shock. Pixel's fine blue skin was now as pale as her own and Score's, and his ears had become rounded instead of pointed. He looked very uncomfortable and depressed.

"You look fine," Score assured him.

"I feel *terrible*," Pixel replied. "No offense, but this skin color is *dreadful*. And my ears feel like they've been sliced in half."

"You'll get used to it," Score promised. He coughed, and his body shook slightly as he turned back to Shanara. "Are we ready for the two transfers now? I'd appreciate getting to Earth as soon as possible."

Helaine realized he must be feeling very sick. "Perhaps you should rest?" she suggested. She couldn't help feeling rather sorry for him. Even if he did drive her crazy a lot of the time.

"The longer I wait, the weaker I get," he said. "We'd better get to Earth while I still have the strength for it."

"Right," Shanara decided. "Let's get on with it. It's time for you to go to New York." She glanced down at her pool. "Please be careful. That place looks like a madhouse."

CHAPTER 3

This place looks like a madhouse, Pixel thought as he stared around their landing zone. Score had worked with Shanara to find a spot in Central Park where they wouldn't be observed materializing out of thin air. That sort of thing, it seemed, wasn't likely to be accepted by the people of the city. They had placed the Portal in a shady grove of trees. The opening vanished behind them as they stepped through, though Pixel knew that Shanara could open it from her end on Treen anytime they called for it. Score then led the way to the edge of the park.

Pixel thought that the park was rather pleasant. So, apparently, did the people of New York, who were out sunbathing, playing with toys or dogs, or just walking or relaxing. Pixel caught Helaine's disapproving frown as she saw some of the immodest clothes the people wore. Well, she was from a world stuck in the Middle Ages where women all wore long, flowing gowns and considered even having their arms bare as the height of immodesty. Seeing Helaine in a T-shirt was astonishing enough, Pixel realized, since she was actually showing her arms.

It was different for him, of course. Clothing styles on his own world were pretty much the same as they were on Earth. At least they were on the friends he'd met in Virtual Reality. Whether he had seen what his friends had actually been wearing, he didn't know, since they could make themselves, their clothes, and their surroundings look like anything they pleased.

As Score had said, there were no blue-skinned people here. It seemed a little odd to Pixel, but it took all kinds of worlds to make a cosmos. The park was fun. It was when they left the park that it became a madhouse.

Helaine gasped and gripped Score's arm tightly as she stared at the road and the surrounding buildings. Tilting back her head she stared up at the skyscrapers with a mixture of astonishment and terror.

"Why don't they fall down?" she asked. "They're so big!"

Score frowned. "They just don't," he answered. "I've never thought about it before. I'm used to it. I guess they don't have skyscrapers where you come from?"

She shook her head, releasing his arm. "The houses are never more than two levels tall," she replied, apparently calming down a bit. "If anyone builds higher, the houses fall over. Obviously, that is not the case here."

"No." Score thought for a minute. "It's something to do with girders and supports," he explained. "They make the buildings stronger. I just don't know how it really works. Maybe Pixel does."

Pixel shook his head. "I've never been that interested in architecture," he admitted. "In my world, it's irrelevant. We can build anything we like in Virtual Reality, so I've no idea how a real house is built." It wasn't the buildings that bothered him: It was the traffic.

The road seemed to be absolutely packed with vehicles of all kinds. Some were obviously for the transportation of people, and others for carrying goods. There were a large number of bright yellow cars. All of the vehicles were moving at great speed, often making loud, irritating honking noises. From time to time, one set of vehicles would stop, and another at right angles to the first would then start moving.

Added to all of the bustle and confusion, there were people everywhere. Some were dressed casually, others in suits. People carried packages, bags, papers, and drinks. It was a whirl of color and movement, one Pixel was not at all used to. He generally spent his time either alone in Virtual Reality, or else with two or three friends. There had to be *hundreds*, if not thousands, of people here!

"How can you stand this?" he demanded.

Score looked puzzled. "Stand what?" he asked.

Gesturing around, Pixel said: "All of this noise and confusion? All of these people and vehicles? It's insane."

That made Score laugh, at least. "It's the greatest city in the world," he replied. "Welcome to New York City."

Helaine shuddered. "And *this* is what you consider to be paradise?" she asked. "It's loud, smelly, and crowded."

"Yes," Score agreed. "Home."

Helaine gave Pixel a look. "No wonder Score is so strange," she commented. "It must be the result of living in this place."

"Knock off the insults," Score growled. He was

still looking pale and tired, and Pixel realized that he had to be under a tremendous strain just to stay on his feet. "Pixel, can you use your ruby to discover where the locket is?" As Pixel's hand went to his pocket, Score grabbed his wrist in a weak grip. "Don't take it out, though. Rubies are pretty valuable here, and someone might decide to steal it."

"How savage," Helaine commented. "Is your property not safe here, then?"

"It's probably safe enough," Score answered. "But there's no point in asking for trouble."

Pixel understood that caution was called for, so he clutched his ruby and tried to focus his powers. For the first time, he realized just how small they were. He had become accustomed to having magical abilities that enabled him to work wonders. Right now, though, he felt as weak as a baby, and he knew that he only possessed a fraction of his normal strength. They were so far out from the center of the Diadem here, magic was really weak.

"I get a very vague feeling that it's south of us," he said finally. "Other than that, I can't get anything. I feel so helpless here."

"Okay," Score said with a sigh. "I guess that means we'd better start looking in the most obvious place — where I used to live. Maybe if we're closer, your magic will work better."

Pixel wasn't sure whether it would or not. "Can you walk that far?" he asked, worried about his friend.

"No, but we don't have to walk," Score answered. He pulled a couple of pieces of paper out of his pocket. "I've got some local money, so we can hop a cab. Stand by the side of the road and hold your arm straight out. One will stop for you."

Pixel did as he was told. He watched the traffic hurtling past, and then one of the yellow cars screeched to a halt beside them. He opened the door and climbed in. Score and Helaine followed. Helaine didn't seem at all happy to be inside the vehicle.

"The Bowery," Score told the driver, who set the car in motion.

Helaine looked as if she was going to be sick. She avoided looking out of the windows, and turned to Score. "You ride inside these things all the time? At this pace?"

"Huh?" Score shrugged. "Sure." He didn't seem to understand her unease.

"Then you are clearly more brave than I had thought," she replied. "I do not like this *hopping a cab*. Are there no horses in this world of yours?"

"Sure." Score gestured out of the window. They were passing the southern edge of Central Park, and Pixel saw carriages being pulled by horses.

"Then why don't we take one of those?" Helaine demanded.

"They don't leave this area," Score answered. "If we want to go downtown, this is the easiest way."

Helaine gritted her teeth. "Then I will endure it. But I will not enjoy it."

Score managed another weak grin. "I told you I'd love to get you onto my world," he said. "Now you can see why I was so bad at riding a horse and all the rest of that medieval stuff of yours."

Helaine shook her head. "No weapons. No horses. All this noise and confusion. What a world!"

The cabdriver must have caught this. He grinned and called back, "She from out of town, man?"

"Yes," Score replied. "*Very* out of town."

Pixel wasn't too disturbed by the ride, and he spent the time studying the city. He'd never been in a place quite like this before. He'd only left his own home once, and that was when he'd been propelled onto the Diadem. His own town was a pleasant place of small houses, each spaced quite a distance from the next. Here, though, the buildings were jammed together, reaching into the sky, and people and vehicles crowded everywhere. Their cab moved in spurts of speed, and then waited while the cross traffic had its turn. It was quite different, and Pixel was rather enjoying it, once he had become accustomed to the crowded conditions.

The buildings were all different shapes and sizes, and some of them were rather attractive. Score spent most of his time almost dozing, but would perk up from time to time and then point out some building or other and identify it. "New York Public Library. Chrysler Building. Empire State Building." None of the names made any sense at all to Pixel, but he accepted that they were obviously places where Score spent a good deal of his time.

Finally, they reached their destination. Score handed over the green paper, and received even more pieces back, which didn't make any sense to Pixel. Then they clambered out of the cab. Helaine almost fell on her knees, and Pixel half expected her to kiss the ground.

"I *hate* those things," she declared. "I am not going in one again. I am quite sore from all the shaking about, and I feel sick."

"Well, it's a good thing we weren't going fast," Score told her. "Then you might have become *really* ill." He turned to Pixel. "Is this any better?"

Pixel gripped his ruby again. Remembering Score's warning, he didn't take it out of his pocket. Once again, he could feel how weak he was. There was just this vague impression again. "It's north of here," he said. "That's all."

"North?" Score questioned. "The apartment where we used to live is a couple of blocks south of here."

"Perhaps the amulet was moved by the person who took it," Pixel suggested. "If we start walking, I'll keep scanning for it. Maybe I'll be able to tell where it is exactly if we get closer to it."

They started walking north. Pixel kept his hand on his ruby, trying to feel where the amulet was. His grasp of the magic was so weak, though, that it would be easy to lose it.

Helaine stared around her as they walked. The buildings here were a lot smaller than the ones she'd seen earlier, and definitely not as well made. Instead of stone and glass, most were in dirty brick colors, and some had been allowed to practically fall apart. There were bags of garbage on the street and litter on the paths. There were even a couple of ill-dressed men sleeping in doorways.

"This place is disgusting," she declared. "Why don't these police of yours make people clean it up?"

"That's not their job," Score answered. "This is a poor section of the city, and the people who live here can't afford to make it much better."

"It's dreadful," Helaine decided. "How can anyone live like this?"

"Sometimes," Score said quietly, "people don't have much choice. It may have been different on your world. After all, you're the daughter of a wealthy lord, and you could get whatever you wanted. This is where I grew up, and it's what I'm used to. I couldn't afford food some days, or a place to sleep. And I had to stay alert *all the time*."

Helaine stared at Score in pity. "It must have been terrible for you," she said gently. "I had no idea. Being forced to live in this squalor . . ."

"Knock off those comments," Score told her. "If other people hear you, they're not going to be as understanding as I am. They might get offended."

That quieted her down for a moment. Then she stiffened and glanced around. "Trouble," she said firmly. Pixel and Score immediately paid attention. Helaine had the ability to sense danger moments before it appeared. Even with her magic reduced, she could still count on that.

For a moment, Pixel saw nothing to worry about. Then six or seven young men moved from out of an alleyway ahead of them. They didn't appear to be armed, but they were clearly dangerous.

"Score," one of them said without warmth or humor. "Good to see you again."

Score scowled. "I doubt that," he spat. "What do you want, Brio?"

Brio raised an eyebrow. He was dressed in blue jeans, with a dark T-shirt that carried some kind of emblem on it, and a leather jacket that had to be uncomfortably hot in this weather. He also wore darkly tinted glasses. "Somebody wants to see you," he replied.

"Tell them to make an appointment with my secretary," Score answered. "I'm kind of busy right now."

"Then I'd advise you to make yourself unbusy," Brio replied. He glanced at Helaine and whistled. "This your secretary, Score? You're moving up in the world. Do you think she'll take some dictation from me?" He grinned, and the other boys with him laughed.

"What I will take from you," Helaine answered coldly, "is blood, if you do not allow us to continue on our way."

Score groaned; obviously he'd been hoping that Helaine would control her temper. Pixel could see why: Antagonizing these people would not be a very smart move.

"Listen to the mouthy chick," Brio said cheerfully. "You've got guts, girlie," he told Helaine. "And talking like that, you're liable to get them spilled on

37

the sidewalk." He drew himself up and stood in front of her. "Now, apologize, or I'll have to get rough."

He'd clearly underestimated Helaine, and Pixel almost felt sorry for him. She glared at the young thug. "I am not *chick* or *girlie*," she answered. "You may call me *my lady* if you have to talk to me at all. But I'd prefer you just to step aside and let us go on our way."

Brio's expression turned livid. "You would, huh? Well, forget it. I'm going to give you —"

Whatever he was offering, he didn't have a chance to continue. He moved forward and Helaine was waiting. She grabbed his wrist, twisted, brought around her foot, and then threw Brio through the air. There was the snap of breaking bones as she let go.

Brio screamed as he hit the sidewalk. He didn't move again, but his six companions did. They all rushed toward Helaine, who was finally smiling.

"I'm starting to like your city after all," she told Score, crouching for the attack.

Score just winced, leaning against the wall. He was definitely not strong enough to help out, so Pixel moved to join Helaine. He was useless at hand-to-hand combat, but he hoped he could still do a little magic.

The lead attacker drew a knife, a wicked-looking blade about eight inches long. Instead of being intimidated, Helaine laughed aloud. "I thought you said that there were no weapons on your world, Score," she called, her eyes sparkling.

"No *legal* ones," Score answered weakly.

"Then I shall take an illegal one," she replied, blocking the boy's lunge with her forearm and deflecting the strike upward. She then kicked her attacker in the stomach, and wrenched the knife from his hand as he fell gasping to the ground. When the third boy approached her with another knife, Helaine used her blade to parry the blow and then sliced him across his upper arm. Screaming, he fell down clutching the wound.

"Back!" one of the remaining four youths yelled. He reached into his jacket and withdrew a small pistol, which he raised at Helaine.

She stared at it, puzzled. "What can that do?" she asked. "It has no blade, nor arrows."

Pixel felt a shock of horror. He kept forgetting that she was from a world without gunpowder. She had no idea what a gun was for, and was simply standing staring at it. With a cry he threw himself against her, shoving her back against the wall.

The gun made an almost deafening noise as it went off. Pixel was terrified for a second that he was going to be killed, but he felt the bullet whip past, barely inches from his head. With shock and relief he realized the youth had missed.

But he still had other bullets.

Helaine had now realized that the pistol was a weapon. Pushing Pixel away, she whipped back her hand and threw the knife hard. The youth screamed as it slammed into his shoulder with such force that it spun him around. The gun went clattering away down the road, and the attacker collapsed, blood oozing from his wound.

But that left Helaine without a weapon, and the others in the gang were no doubt armed. It would only be a moment before they attacked again. Pixel braced himself, trying to focus on making fire. If he could set the attackers' clothing alight, it would help. But he wasn't sure he had the magical strength.

There came the sound of a siren. It had to be the signal for a truce or something, because when they heard it, the gang members ignored their victims. They scooped up Brio and the other two whom Helaine had wounded, and retreated.

Helaine was grinning, happy again. She loved to fight, and this had been her idea of fun. It was Pixel's idea of something to avoid, of course, and he was glad that it was over. He went to join Score, who was barely able to stand up. As he did so, a blue vehicle whirled around the corner, and skidded to a halt beside them.

Two men dressed in blue uniforms jumped out

and both pulled out guns. "Okay," one of them said. "Up against the wall, quick."

Helaine glared at them. "More thugs," she growled. "Don't worry. I can take them."

"No," Score protested. "These are the police. Don't fight them."

"Oh." Helaine stared at the two men. "The lord's retainers? Then why are they threatening us?"

"Against the wall!" The first policeman repeated. "This is your last warning."

"Do as they say," Score insisted.

Pixel obeyed, but Helaine looked ready to fight. However, she copied Score, facing the wall with her hands up. One of the policemen then searched them quickly. Helaine gave a shriek of protest and almost punched him out. She calmed down only when Score shook his head.

"Right, into the car," the man ordered.

"We do not need to hop a cab," Helaine said stiffly, glaring at him. "We will walk wherever we're going."

The policeman glowered at her. "You'll do as you're told, girlie," he informed her. "Into the car, and no more wisecracks."

Score put a hand on Helaine's arm. "Please," he begged. "Just do as they say. We're in enough trouble as it is."

"Why are we in trouble?" asked Helaine, puzzled. "We did nothing wrong."

"But they don't know that," Score explained. "Come on, please?"

"Very well," Helaine said, sniffing. "But I will tell you once again that I do not like this world of yours too much."

"Relax," Score muttered. "I have a suspicion the feeling's mutual."

CHAPTER 4

Score was exhausted, and being booked at the local precinct house wasn't helping his mood much. He could tell that his strength was being drained, and he didn't think he had a great deal of time left before it would kill him. Even walking was causing him pain. Unfortunately, the police weren't very sympathetic.

"Gang warfare," the booking sergeant grunted, glaring at them. "Why don't you young idiots get real lives?"

"This is my real life," Pixel answered, puzzled. Score winced. The police, naturally, thought Pixel was being sarcastic, and that didn't improve their mood.

"Maybe I should answer most of the questions," Score suggested. "You two aren't really up on what they're talking about." He turned to the sergeant. "My friends are from out of town," he explained. "We were attacked by a gang. We're not part of a gang ourselves. We just defended ourselves, that's all."

"So you say," the sergeant growled. He peered at Score. "What's wrong with you? Are you on something?"

"No," Score answered. "Though I'm starting to wish I had some medicine. I'm just sick."

The sergeant's scowl softened a bit at this. "We'll see about getting you a doctor, then," he conceded. "Just as soon as we've booked you in. Now, name?" He was typing this into a computer.

Ouch. Score couldn't answer that one honestly. If he gave his real name — Matt Caruso — then the computer was bound to tell the policeman that Matt Caruso had run away from Child Protective Services, and he'd be returned to them again. There was no way he was going back there. On the other hand, the police might just find the record anyway, whether he cooperated or not. What to do? If he hesitated too long, the cop was going to get suspicious. "Score," he finally said.

"That's not a name," the policeman said. "That's a gang name. What's your *real* name?"

"Score," he insisted.

The policeman sighed. "You're determined to

44

make this hard on yourself, aren't you? Okay, what about personal details? Address? Any relatives in town?"

Score could imagine what the response would be if he answered that one honestly! *Yes, my father's Bad Tony Caruso, currently in prison.* No way. He shook his head. "I told you, we just got into town. We were going to look for a place to stay."

"Then where are you from?" the sergeant asked. "Before you came into town?"

"Treen," said Pixel helpfully. Score groaned.

"Queens?" the cop asked, misunderstanding the answer. "What street?"

"You wouldn't know it," Score insisted. "Look, we didn't do anything, and all we want is to be let go. We've got things to take care of."

"I'm sure you do. And so do I." The sergeant looked at Helaine. "Come on, you seem like a nice kid. What's your name?"

Helaine had obviously caught on that it wasn't wise to give her true name. "Renald," she answered. "And I am *not* a kid. I am the daughter of a lord."

"She's from out of town all right," the sergeant decided. "English, huh? That explains her snooty attitude."

Score held out a hand, which shook no matter how hard he tried to hide it. "Please," he urged Helaine, before she exploded again. "Just let me do this, okay?"

She glared at him. "I had thought that these police of yours were supposed to enforce the laws. Why, then, are we imprisoned while the people who attacked us without provocation are still free?"

The sergeant sighed. "Look, missy, we've got men out looking for them. But I doubt we'll find them. In the meantime, we've only got your word that you're innocent."

"And you doubt my word?" Helaine was getting really incensed. "I demand to meet the lord you serve! I shall insist that he flog you for insulting a noble like that!"

To Score's relief, the cop laughed at this and then grinned at Score. "Is she always this bad?" he asked.

"No," Score answered. "Usually she's worse."

The sergeant chuckled and then turned to Pixel. "I don't suppose you have an honest-to-goodness name either?"

"It's Pixel," he answered seriously.

"Great." The sergeant shrugged. "A kid who doesn't do drugs, a dame with an attitude, and now a pixie. What did I ever do to deserve this?" He looked hard at them. "I'm holding you overnight," he told them. "If there's no evidence against you by the morning, you can all go." He gestured to his desk. "Now, empty your pockets."

Helaine shook her head. "What I own is none of your business," she said.

The sergeant sighed again. "Look, we can do this the easy way or the hard way. You can either empty your pockets willingly, or else I'll have a couple of officers do it for you. Take your pick."

Helaine looked as if she were going to argue again, but then she looked at Score. He knew he had to be a sight right now. It was all he could do to stand up. She gritted her teeth and emptied her pockets onto the desk. Score and Pixel followed her.

The sergeant and both policemen whistled and stared at the pile of gemstones. "You three have been on a spree, haven't you?" the sergeant said. "Where did you get those?"

"They were given to us," Pixel replied. "They're *ours*."

"You're a little young to own a fortune in jewels, kid," the sergeant answered. "You must have stolen them from somewhere."

"No, we didn't," Score said. He'd been trying to stay calm, but it was getting harder for him. "I'm willing to bet you don't have any reports of missing jewels that match those. They're ours, and you'd better take good care of them. We want them back when you let us out of here." He swayed, and then fell into the closest chair. "Now, will you just lock us up? I need a rest."

One of the policemen felt for his pulse. "It's erratic," he announced. "You'd better call a doctor, fast."

Score was glad that they were finally doing something right. It wasn't their fault that they couldn't figure out what to do with three magic-users, of course, but it was frustrating. The problem was, there really wasn't much a doctor could do for him. They simply *had* to find the amulet.

Bad Tony steepled his hands and leaned forward over his desk, staring at Brio. The young man was pale and battered. At least it proved he had been trying to do his job. "I sent you to bring me my son," Tony said coldly. "You're here, but my son isn't. So where is he?"

Brio swallowed nervously. He knew that it was not a smart move to get on the bad side of Tony Caruso, and he obviously didn't have good news. "With the police," he replied. "They came when they heard gunshots."

"And how did that happen?" Tony demanded. "There should have been no need for guns. My son is a coward. I was certain he would cave in and come with you."

"It wasn't him," Brio said. "There were a couple of other kids with him. One of them was a really good fighter." He paused and licked his lips. "She fought us off."

"She?" echoed Bad Tony, astonished. "You mean some *girl* beat up you and Johnny, and put Dave in the hospital?"

Brio looked utterly miserable, but he knew better than to lie to his boss. "Yes."

"Terrific." Tony scowled, thinking furiously. There had to be some way to salvage this operation. He could do nothing himself, since the police were still actively looking for him. Which left him only one choice: He had to inform Mr. Toshiro. The businessman didn't have a record, and he would be able to free Score from jail. After that, Tony could act. He looked up at Brio. "Get out," he said, disgusted. "You're lucky I'm in a good mood. I'm going to be reunited with my son, and family occasions always bring out the best in me. But one more mistake and they'll be forwarding your mail to the bottom of the East River. You understand me?"

Brio nodded, then beat a hasty retreat.

Bad Tony reached for the phone and dialed a number he had memorized. He had to get the wheels moving as soon as possible. What he had planned couldn't wait for very much longer.

The doctor had given Score a shot, and then left him and Pixel alone in a small holding cell. To Score's surprise, whatever he'd been injected with seemed to have helped a little. His head was fuzzy, but he didn't feel quite as weak. Pixel sat beside him, obviously worried.

"How are you feeling?" he asked sympathetically.

"A little better," Score answered. "But it's some kind of medicine high, not a cure. The magical attack is getting worse." He didn't have the strength or the wits to lie about his condition. "If we don't get that locket back by tomorrow morning, I'm going to be dead."

"And we're stuck in *here*," Pixel fumed, slamming his hand on the bars of the cell. "And they separated us from Helaine. If we were all together, we might be able to plan an escape."

Score laughed. It was a thin and watery laugh, but he couldn't help being amused by Pixel. "Pix, she's a *girl*. They don't lock girls and guys together in New York. It's not considered polite."

"Then we have to get out of here on our own," Pixel said firmly. "It's up to me to come up with a plan."

"Good luck," Score replied, and then lay back, trying to conserve his strength. His body felt terribly weak, and his pulse was racing. It was as if he were on the edge of a huge, swirling whirlpool that would sooner or later suck him in. He was going around the edge, not quite lost but far too close for comfort.

"Well," said Oracle's familiar voice, "I have to say that the three of you have the most amazing ability to end up imprisoned. Is it a hobby?"

Score groaned. "Don't you ever turn up when you could actually be some sort of help?" he asked. "I'm willing to bet you're here with some dire warning as usual."

"Then you'd be wrong," Oracle answered rather smugly. "I'm here because Shanara's been able to discover something. The problem is that she can't understand it. Maybe you can." This is what she saw in her scrying pool.

A piece of paper appeared in front of them with these symbols:

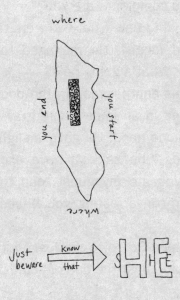

As Oracle vanished, Score lay back. "About as much use as always," he grumbled. "If he'd only brought a hacksaw in a cake or something." The humor was lost on Pixel, of course. "Now, I just want to rest."

The door leading to the main part of the police station opened, and the booking sergeant walked through.

Score groaned. "Can't I get any rest at all?" he demanded.

The sergeant had his keys out and was unlocking the cell. "Why didn't you tell me that you were the guests of Toshiro Corporation?" he asked. He looked worried. "This was all a mistake, right? You aren't going to file a complaint, are you?"

"I might, if I knew what you were talking about," Score replied foggily. He managed to sit up, with Pixel's help. "What's going on?"

There was another man in the doorway. He was Asian, dressed in an impeccable gray suit, and carried a hat in one hand. He gave a slight formal bow. "My apologies," he said. "I have explained to the police that you are my guest, and they have realized their error in arresting you. Please, come with me."

Pixel helped Score to his feet, but the sergeant shook his head. "Just the one of you," he said.

Score shook his head and then wished he hadn't. It took a minute for him to stop feeling dizzy. "Then I'm not going," he said. "It's all three of us, or none of us." This seemed to puzzle the stranger. "And I'm not going anywhere until I talk to him, anyway."

The sergeant seemed to be upset at this demand, but he looked at the man for a clue as to what to do. "It's very irregular," he complained.

"The boy is, as you can see, in need of medical assistance," the man said politely. "It may be that he is a trifle confused. Would you allow me to speak with him alone for a moment?"

The policeman hesitated, and then shrugged. He backed off down the corridor, keeping the cell in his sight. The man stepped into the cell.

"Who the heck are you?" Score demanded in a low voice. "I'm not going with anyone I don't know and trust, even if it gets me out of here."

"I am Toshiro," the man replied. "The head of Toshiro Corporation. I need your help, Mr. Caruso. And I am in a position to help you in return." He leaned forward and said softly, "I know where the amulet is."

Score stared at him in surprise. Maybe he *would* be saved, after all. "What do you know about it?"

"That without it you will die," Toshiro answered. "Now, please come with me and I will be able to help you."

Score nodded. He didn't know what this man really wanted, but if it led them to the locket, then he had no choice but to agree. "Only Pixel and Helaine must come with me," he insisted. "All three of us, or I stay here."

Toshiro looked frustrated, but then he nodded. "Agreed." He turned and snapped his fingers for the sergeant.

Score sighed, and settled back. Let Toshiro work out the details. At least this meant they were getting out of jail. And, apparently, on the trail of the locket. He wished he knew who this Toshiro guy was, and what he really wanted, but for the moment he had to trust the man.

He could only pray he wasn't making a huge mistake.

CHAPTER 5

Helaine couldn't understand why Score thought so highly of this planet of his. She had been here just a few hours, and so far nothing good had come of it. Being locked in a small cell with two strange women had done nothing either to calm her down or relieve her fears about Score. The two women with her were obviously used to this routine and stayed out of her way, which suited Helaine fine. It gave her more time to think and plan an escape.

The problem was, she was too worried about Score. He had been looking really ill when these police people had forcibly separated her from her two friends. A tough-looking policewoman had insisted that Helaine could not stay with Pixel and Score. Now all Helaine could do was to worry.

Her powers were very weak on Earth, but she managed to conjure up a small flame while she had her back to her cellmates. With time she hoped to melt the lock of her cell, but it would be best to wait until everyone went to sleep before trying this. But how long could she afford to stay here with Score so sick?

Then the policewoman returned, looking slightly embarrassed. She unlocked the cell, and nodded to Helaine. "Come on," she said. "We're letting you go. Why didn't any of you tell us you were with the Toshiro Corporation?"

Helaine didn't know what the woman meant, but she didn't intend to let on. "You deserve to be told nothing," she said haughtily. "The way that you have treated me . . ."

"Oh, great," muttered the policewoman. "I smell a lawsuit."

Again, Helaine didn't know what the woman was talking about. But she had discovered a long time ago that if you were aristocratic enough, nobody asked you to explain anything. She strode down the corridor toward the exit without waiting for the woman to catch up to her.

When they were back at the sergeant's desk she

saw that Score and Pixel were already there, accompanied by a stranger. Pixel was supporting Score, who definitely looked worse than he had before. She hurried over to them.

"He's getting weaker," Pixel confirmed. "But Mr. Toshiro says he knows where the amulet is."

Hope began to flood back into Helaine. She hadn't wanted to admit it even to herself, but she had started to brace herself for the thought that they might not be able to save Score's life. Now she was so relieved that they were on the right track at last. "Hold on, Score," she encouraged him. "We'll save you."

"You'd better," he muttered. "Or I promise I'll come back and haunt you worse than Oracle does."

He still had his strange sense of humor, at least. Helaine turned to the sergeant and held out her hand. "We will take back our gems now," she stated. The sergeant nodded, and handed over three padded envelopes marked with their names.

"They're all there," he assured her.

"I will check that," Helaine replied with a sniff that showed precisely what she thought of his assurances. But he was right, and their belongings were untouched. She pocketed her own four gems, and slipped Score's into his pockets. Pixel took his own.

"Now we must be out of here," Mr. Toshiro announced. "Do you require help with Mr. Caruso?"

It took Helaine a moment to realize that *Mr. Caruso* was actually Score. "No," she answered. "He's our friend. We'll manage." She took one of Score's arms and helped Pixel to lift him up. Together, they followed the stranger out of the police station and to a waiting vehicle.

This was a large black machine, at least three times the size of the cab they had ridden in earlier. Its windows were tinted the same shade of black, and a man in livery stood beside the open door at the back. Helaine didn't have to know very much about this world to realize that Toshiro was clearly a man of some importance — perhaps even a minor lord. It explained this expensive vehicle and the deference the police had shown him. It seemed as though, somehow, they had acquired the support of one of the local leaders of this strange community.

Inside, the car was vastly more luxurious than the cab had been. There were two sets of very comfortable seats facing each another. Pixel and Helaine laid Score out on the back seat, and Helaine sat with his head in her lap.

"I could get to like this style of travel," Score managed to joke. "You've got a very nice lap. Cozy."

"Don't get too used to it," she warned him, feeling her face burn in embarrassment. "You won't be traveling like this again."

"Then I promise to enjoy it as much as possible this time," he told her. His eyes closed, and he seemed to drift into sleep. Helaine brushed his hair back, out of his eyes. She wasn't sure how she felt exactly, but she knew that she didn't want to lose him, no matter how irritating he could be.

From where Mr. Toshiro sat, he studied them. After the liveried servant closed the door, he went to the front of the car and started it up.

Helaine had not enjoyed the cab ride at all, but this was very different. For one thing, the windows cut down on the glare from the city, as well as most of the noise. For another, this car was much smoother and gentler. And, finally, there was a lead on the amulet at last.

Pixel leaned forward from where he sat at Score's feet. "You said you know about the locket," he prompted their host.

Mr. Toshiro nodded. "Indeed I do. I do not have it myself, but I have an idea as to where it is."

"What do you know about the locket?" demanded Helaine. She was glad to be out of the jail, but was still not sure she was ready to trust their rescuer. "And why are you helping us?"

"I know that it is enchanted," their host replied.

"It is being used to drain the life force from your young friend. If you do not find it, he will die." He smiled slightly. "Unlike most people on this planet, I accept that magic is real, and that this is being done by magic. As to why I am helping you . . ." He shrugged. "Partly it is because you need help. Partly it is because I, in turn, require your assistance."

"Ah." Pixel nodded. "So you want us to do something for you in return for your help."

"Precisely," Toshiro agreed. "A trade to benefit us both." He nodded to the sleeping Score. "Especially, I think, Mr. Caruso."

"Fair enough," agreed Helaine. "But how is it that you know all of this? Score told us that most people on Earth don't know anything about magic."

"I am a . . . curious person," Toshiro answered. "I do not believe that everything can be explained by science, though certainly science has its uses." He gestured around them. "I have made a great success in the business world through technology. I am very wealthy and can have almost anything my heart desires. Except for the one thing that I want the most. That remains out of reach of science.

"But not of magic." He leaned forward. "Knowing that I needed a fresh approach to my problem, I studied magic. Alas, I do not myself possess the talents to actually perform magic, but I know that it is a real phenomenon. I have . . . certain people in my employ who can use it. But their power is very limited. Still, they were able to locate a strong source of magic for me — this amulet that you seek. And they were able to inform me that its owner had a tremendous amount of magic at his disposal." He nodded at Score. "Mr. Caruso there. So I decided that I should have to meet Mr. Caruso when he inevitably returned home. You see, we discovered that someone had magically poisoned the amulet to lure Mr. Caruso back to Earth from wherever he was. All I needed to do was to intercept him before his unknown foe could find him."

Pixel nodded. "I'm beginning to understand some of this," he said. He looked at Helaine. "Those street thugs we ran into must have been employed by the person who has the amulet, and they were trying to capture Score. Mr. Toshiro found us before our unknown magician did."

It made sense, but Helaine was still not sure she trusted the man. She reached out with what little magic she still retained and checked him out. She discovered that he was telling at least some of the truth. There was no touch of magic about him, so he was certainly not the wizard who was poisoning Score. But there was a trace of residual magic, which made sense if, as he claimed, he employed magicians to work for him.

"What is this *problem* of yours?" Helaine prompted him.

"It must wait for a short while," the businessman answered. "You will understand it better if you see it. And, I trust, you will feel compassion. It will not take us long to reach my home, I assure you. The slight delay will not injure Mr. Caruso further."

Helaine felt a slight tingling in her mind, and then she realized that it had to be Pixel trying to talk to her telepathically. Something he didn't want Toshiro to hear. . . . She felt for her agate gemstone to enable her to make the link. It wasn't as clear as normal, but at least she could manage it. *What is it?* she asked him.

He doesn't know that the two of us can do magic, too, Pixel explained. *He thinks it's just Score. I don't see any reason to make him think otherwise, do you?*

Smart! *No,* she agreed. *It's better if he underestimates us. He *may* be telling the truth, but I'd like to be sure of that before we start trusting him.*

She broke off contact, and, to make it seem as if she'd only been thinking to herself, asked, "Where is your home? In this city?"

"No," Toshiro replied. "It's on Long Island."

"An island?" Helaine asked. "Is that far from here?"

Their host laughed. "You are obviously not a local," he replied. "New York City *is* an island. Long Island is joined to it. The trip there will take us about fifteen minutes, once we reach my heliport."

Helaine had no idea what a *heliport* might be, but she found the idea that they were already on an island interesting. It made sense, since towns on islands were easier to defend from enemies. Long Island was probably an ally of New York, then.

The car stopped, and the door beside her opened. Another uniformed man held the door while Mr. Toshiro stepped out. Pixel and Helaine managed to move Score from the car. He didn't even wake up.

There was a wheelchair awaiting them and Mr. Toshiro gestured at it. "It will be easier to transport him in this," he suggested. "Though we do not have far to go."

Helaine lowered Score into the chair, and he woke slightly. "Are we there yet?" he muttered.

"Almost," Mr. Toshiro replied. "Rest for now."

"Okay," he agreed, and fell asleep again.

Helaine pushed the chair and followed Mr. Toshiro. They were beside a river on some long, flat, stonelike ground. There were several other cars parked, and people hurrying around. There were also two strange machines, one of which seemed to have sprung to life. Helaine had never seen anything like it before.

It looked vaguely like a very large car, though the wheels it rested on were stalklike. There was a glass-covered cabin with several doors behind it, one of which was open. A man in strange headgear ushered them toward it. The oddest part of the machine was that on its top there were four long, narrow blades that looked to Helaine like a windmill that had fallen on its back. The machine was making an even louder noise than the cars had earlier.

Mr. Toshiro clambered inside and beckoned for them to follow. A pretty young woman and a man helped to get Score into one of the seats. Puzzled, Helaine followed and strapped herself into another seat as she was told. Why had they moved from one car to another? It didn't make any sense to her. The young woman joined them, and then the man shut the door, enclosing them all inside the odd car.

"Prepare for takeoff," the young woman said pleasantly.

"Takeoff?" Helaine asked, confused. "I'm not taking anything off! I've got little enough on as it is."

The woman looked totally confused, but Mr. Toshiro found the whole thing very amusing. "She doesn't mean for you to take anything off," he explained. "It is the helicopter that will be taking off momentarily."

"Helicopter?" Helaine asked. She wished she knew what all of this was about. "What is that?"

"It's what we're in," Pixel explained. "It flies."

"Flies?" Helaine was starting to get alarmed. "But it has no wings or feathers. It's not even a dragon! How can it fly?"

The whole world lurched under her. There was a terrible noise overhead, which she realized had to be coming from the windmill blades. Then the ground dropped away.

She felt as if she was going to be sick. Her eyes widened as she stared out of the windows and watched the city fall away. She covered her mouth and held the contents of her stomach in place by sheer force of will. The young woman handed her a bag of some sort.

"Just in case," the woman said. Then, to Pixel, she added, "Hasn't she flown before?"

"Oh, yes," he assured her. "Just never in a machine. I don't think she likes it."

Mr. Toshiro raised an eyebrow. "Interesting. So she *is* from another world, then?"

Pixel nodded. "Where dragons and rocs fly. But not machines."

"This can't possibly fly," Helaine stated, trying not to look at the land passing below them. "It is far too heavy and has no wings."

"It *is* flying," Pixel assured her. "And it's very safe. Don't worry."

"That's easy for you to say," Helaine complained, as her stomach rebelled further. It was one thing to levitate herself and fly using magic, but magic on Earth wasn't strong enough for her to do that. There was no way that this *helicopter* could stay in the air! Helaine was sure it was bound to crash and kill them all.

She had not felt this sick or miserable for a long time.

CHAPTER 6

Pixel didn't have the nerve to confess to Helaine that this was his first helicopter ride, too. He'd done plenty of "flying" in Virtual Reality, but never physically. On the other hand, since he was from a world even more technologically advanced than Earth, he could accept it and take it in his stride.

He found the flight fascinating, and spent most of it staring out the windows at the ground below. He imagined that this New York had to be a fairly large place even on Earth, because it seemed to be back-to-back buildings for the entire time. As Toshiro had promised, the flight lasted barely fifteen minutes before the machine settled down on a concrete pad close to a large house overlooking a bay. The view was beautiful, especially since the weather was so nice. The gardens of the house had been immaculately landscaped, and the whole place reeked of wealth and power.

Helaine was the first out, eagerly leaving the vehicle. She and Pixel watched as the young woman and a man who had met the helicopter helped the sleeping Score into the wheelchair again.

"I'm glad he didn't see me," Helaine muttered to Pixel. "He'd never let me forget it if he knew how scared I was." She glared at him. "Don't you dare breathe a word about it!"

Pixel blushed slightly. "Of course not," he promised.

Toshiro had joined them, and he gestured for them to follow him. "My aide will bring your friend," he told them.

"No," Helaine said very firmly. "*I* will bring our friend."

Toshiro bowed slightly. "As you wish."

Pixel realized that Helaine was still very cautious about trusting their host, and wanted to keep Score close to her. He felt a pang of jealousy about this, but then rebuked himself for feeling that way. Helaine was just looking after Score. There was nothing more to read into it.

Toshiro led the way toward the house through the beautiful gardens. There was a large pond beside the path, with a waterfall at the far end. Pixel saw the flicker of color below the water and realized it was stocked with fish. Carefully tended plants and trees gave the area a lovely look.

The house was only two stories high, with sleek lines and large windows. It had to be big enough to hold at least fifty people, but there was no way of telling just how many were really there. Pixel was still unused to the real world. How many people would it take to run a place like this?

Pixel found the inside of the house to be as rich as the exterior. There were works of art, subtle but significant, showing taste as well as money. The furniture was functional and spread out carefully to allow plenty of room for the wheelchair. The young woman from the helicopter vanished, leaving them alone with their host.

"As I promised you earlier," Toshiro told Pixel and Helaine, "I will now explain the nature of my problem. As you can see, I am a wealthy and powerful man." He gestured around the room. "Whatever I wish, within limits, I can have. But what I want the most, I am denied."

Pixel narrowed his eyes and studied the man. "So what do you want from us?" he asked suspiciously.

"Nothing harmful, I assure you," Toshiro answered. "Your friend Score is able to perform magic, is he not?"

"Yes," Pixel confirmed. Toshiro already knew at least that much.

"What I require is for him to do one small task for me."

"If it's so small," Helaine asked suspiciously, "why can't one of your own magicians do the trick?"

"Because they are not that strong," Toshiro explained. "Oh, they were able to trace Score and find out about the amulet for me. But beyond that, they are virtually powerless. Since Score was able to cross from Earth to another world and bring you back with him, I imagine he must be a lot more powerful than they are. What is beyond their abilities should be within his grasp."

"Perhaps," agreed Pixel with a shrug. "But we need to know what you want before we can tell you whether or not he can manage it."

Toshiro nodded. "Please, wake him up and I will show you the nature of my problem."

Helaine hesitated, but then bent down to shake Score. "Wake up," she murmured. "It's time to get to work."

Score shook his head and then opened his eyes,

which were red-rimmed and unfocused. "Oh, great. Just what I need in this condition."

"We don't have a lot of choice," Pixel told him. "Mr. Toshiro has offered to help us track down the locket if you help him first."

"Well, that's something, at any rate." Score sighed, and struggled to sit upright. "I feel so drained, though. Can I sit this one out?"

"You're just trying to make me do all the work," Helaine complained. "But I suppose so." She pushed him along after Toshiro, while Pixel brought up the rear. They went down a long corridor and into another room.

Pixel's eyes widened as he looked around. There was a large mainframe computer, and several work-stations around the room. It was, he realized, probably state-of-the-art equipment for this world. It looked like an antique to him, but he knew it had to be very powerful.

There was one person in the room waiting for them. A girl. Pixel immediately realized why there had been plenty of room for Score's wheelchair: The girl was in one of her own. She was petite and dark-haired, very pretty and about Pixel's own age. It was clear that she was quite dependent on her wheelchair.

"My daughter, Destiny," Toshiro explained, and he introduced the three of them to her.

Destiny gave a slight bow of her head. "I am pleased to meet you," she informed them. She saw Pixel glance admiringly about the room. "You like my playthings?"

"It's quite a setup," he said with a smile. "You must be able to do a lot with this."

"I can do more with this equipment than most research universities," Destiny said proudly. Then she scowled. "Except the one thing that I most desire — escape from my prison."

Pixel couldn't help feeling sorry for her. To be trapped like she was couldn't be easy for anyone, especially someone as adventurous as Destiny appeared to be. "I'm sorry about that," he told her honestly. "Isn't there any medical help for you?"

"No," Toshiro said. "And, believe me, if there was, I would have gladly paid for it. *This* is what my money cannot buy me: my daughter's freedom to move about as she desires."

Score managed a very weak laugh. "*That's* what you want us to do?" he asked. "Cure Destiny?" He tapped his own chest with a shaking hand. "Trust me, if any of us had any healing ability, I wouldn't be in this shape right now."

Pixel winced. Score had been asleep when he and

Helaine had agreed that they would keep their powers quiet. As he feared, Toshiro's brow furrowed. "You are *all* magicians?" he asked.

Destiny stared at them, and Pixel could feel the stirrings of magic in the air. "Yes, they are," she breathed.

"And so are you," Pixel answered, knowing she was the one who had made the magic stir. "Your father neglected to mention that."

"There did not seem to be any point," Toshiro answered. "I assume your own . . . oversight was for the same reason."

"Three magicians," Destiny said, a terrible longing in her voice. "Well, perhaps none of you alone can help me, but all three of you and my own small contribution might, surely?"

Pixel didn't want to raise her hopes any further. "I don't know," he said, speaking frankly. "Healing isn't one of our talents. We've never really tried it."

"Please!" Destiny begged. "You must help me! You're my only chance. And then I can help you in seeking out Score's amulet to cure him."

Pixel didn't know what to say. He exchanged a glance with Helaine, and saw that the same thought must have crossed her mind. If there was a chance of helping Score, they *had* to try it. "I think we could use some advice," Pixel finally said. He held in his mind the calling spell, one of the very first they had ever learned, and then summoned Oracle by reciting his name backward.

"Well, this is an improvement on that jail cell," Oracle remarked, looking around the room. "You seem to be moving up in the world."

"It may not be *their* jail cell," Destiny commented. "But it's certainly *mine*."

Oracle raised an eyebrow. "Making new friends as usual?" he asked pleasantly.

"She needs our help," Pixel explained.

"Ah." Oracle nodded. "A personality transplant, I take it?"

"She wants us to heal her," Helaine said.

"We thought you might know if this is possible," Pixel added. "We've never tried to do anything like it." He spread his hands helplessly. "And Helaine couldn't bring her Book of Magic with her, so we can't even check for new spells."

"You have a book of spells?" Destiny asked, obviously impressed. "Ones that actually *work*?" She gave a sharp laugh. "I've read plenty here on Earth that claim to work, but they never do."

"These do," Helaine admitted. "But I don't remember there being any healing spells."

Oracle shook his head. "Healing is a rare art," he replied. "Not many magicians can do it." He crossed to Destiny's wheelchair and bent to examine her legs. "Simple stuff, sure, no problem. Speeding up a cut so that it heals or mending broken bones isn't too hard. It's a matter of manipulating time mostly, so it takes two minutes instead of two months. But curing someone who can't walk isn't that simple." He glanced up. "How long have you been like this?"

"Since I was born," she said bitterly. "I've never been able to walk."

"Then speeding up time isn't going to do the slightest bit of good," Oracle announced. "There's nothing there for it to work on. If they are going to help you, it'll have to be some other way." He stood up. "Well, it's out of my depth, so I'd better go and get an expert opinion. If it's possible, Shanara should know about it. I'll be back when I have an answer." He promptly vanished.

Toshiro raised an eyebrow. "Is he always like that?"

"Always," Pixel confirmed. "You get used to it eventually."

"He seemed rather rude," Destiny commented.

"That's just his way," Score told her. "Look, if you don't mind, I'm just going to doze awhile, to conserve my strength. There's not much I can do right now, anyway." His eyes closed again.

Pixel and Helaine exchanged worried looks.

Score was clearly getting worse, and they were no closer to finding the locket and curing him. Pixel decided it was time to get tough. "Look," he said bluntly to Destiny, "as you've seen, we're trying to help you. Now, isn't it about time you helped us a bit in return? What do you know about the amulet?"

Destiny nodded. "Of course. Let's use the time wisely while we're waiting for Oracle. Come here." She gestured to her computer screen. Pixel drew closer, as did Helaine.

"What is that thing?" she asked, staring at the screen.

"A computer," Destiny answered. "Haven't you ever seen one before?"

"She's from a world that's still medieval," Pixel explained. "All of this stuff is completely new to her."

"Oh." Destiny chewed her lip for a moment. "I guess this is a bit like a seeing pool, where you can call up whatever you want on a screen instead of water. Only it works because of science, not magic. It's very useful." She tapped a couple of keys, and a picture sprang to life. It showed a small silver locket. "This is what you need to find. I managed to make an image of it after viewing it magically." She sighed in frustration. "I *know* it's around somewhere in the area. Somewhere in New York. I just don't know where. I've used my magical skills and my computer, and all I get is an idea that it's around. Take a look."

"It doesn't make a lot of sense," agreed Pixel. "But magic's like that sometimes. It can get very frustrating." Without letting anyone know what he was doing, Pixel closed his hand around the ruby in his pocket and concentrated on the image of the locket. Again, he could only sense that it was reasonably close, and to the west. Obviously, as Destiny had guessed, it was in New York somewhere.

"Did you miss me?" Oracle asked as he entered the room again. "Well, I've possibly got some good news for you. There *may* be a way to cure Destiny. Perhaps even two ways."

"Two?" Destiny sat upright, her face eager. "One will do! Tell me!"

"It's nice to have an enthusiastic audience," Oracle said appreciatively. "Well, the easiest way is a healing spell. I wasn't sure that there was an appropriate one, but Shanara knew one." He held up a sheet of paper with the spell written out on it for them to read. "Theoretically, it should work. Practically . . ." He spread his hands. "The problem is that it takes a lot of magical energy. Neither Shanara nor I could be certain that you'd have enough power on Earth for this to work. The only way to know would be to try it."

"It's worth a try, surely?" Pixel asked.

"Definitely!" Destiny eagerly agreed .

Helaine held up her hand. "What about the second way?" she asked.

"Oh, that." Oracle grinned. "The same thing, only this time on Treen. If you moved there through a Portal, then your power levels would increase, and you should have enough to effect a cure."

Destiny frowned. "Well, if you're sure that would work, why not simply do that instead?"

"Because it will only work on Treen," Oracle explained. "If you were then to return to Earth, you'd resume your current condition. So, if we were to do that, you'd have to become an exile from Earth." He gestured around. "Could you give up all of this so easily?"

"To be free at last?" Destiny asked. "Easily. To be able to walk, dance, jump . . . *anything* would be worth it."

"Also," Oracle added, "there's no guarantee that you would survive the trip *to* Treen. Your magical abilities might not be powerful enough."

"Well, let's try it here first," Pixel said. "Going to Treen can be our backup plan. We'd have to go to Central Park, anyway, where the Portal is." He looked at Helaine and then Destiny. "Did you both memorize the spell?" They nodded. "Good. Then let's link up our powers and see if we're strong enough for it." He held out a hand to each girl. They gripped him, and then each other. "Focus!" he commanded.

It was very strange doing this with Destiny instead of Score. Linking up in the past had seemed almost natural, the easiest thing in the worlds. Now, though, it felt slightly unbalanced. Pixel could feel Destiny's personality, very different from Score's, as part of the merger. They were connected magically. Pixel could feel the magic build.

Destiny was definitely gifted, but she was not as strong as Score. However, she was definitely stronger than Score was at this moment. Pixel felt the magic growing and flowing about them as he began to recite the words of the spell. *Senoj ados oc.* The words took shape and form, and he could feel the power starting to flow. It was as if he were being drained into Destiny's legs. He could almost see the nerves, the blood vessels, and the long-useless muscles. It was like a dark pit down which they were pouring the light of magic, to illuminate and strengthen what was there.

He could feel the muscles start to tense, as power flowed into them for the first time. There was a tingling throughout her limbs as Destiny concentrated.

Pixel opened his eyes, the power still moving within him. He looked down at Destiny's legs.

Her toes were twitching slightly. She stared at them in awe. "It's working," she breathed. "I can feel my toes."

"Good," Helaine said. "Then the spell is doing its job."

"Perhaps," Pixel cautioned them. "But it may not be quite enough. It's drained all of my strength for a while. But try to walk and see what happens."

Destiny nodded eagerly. She pushed back the blanket covering her. She had shorts on underneath it, showing off her long legs. Her skin was pale, but the muscle tone looked good. She gripped the arms of her chair, and pushed herself upward, strain and hope on her face. Her legs connected with the carpet, and she grunted as she struggled to stand up. Pixel wanted to help her, but knew that he shouldn't. She had to try this alone.

Slowly she managed to struggle upright, and then stood there, wobbling slightly, her eyes wild with excitement. "It's working!" she breathed. "I'm standing up! I'm —"

Her legs buckled, and she fell forward with a cry of disappointment and rage. Pixel and Helaine managed to grab her before she slammed into the floor. They lowered her gently back into her wheelchair. Pixel could feel the shock and anger coursing through her body.

"It *failed*!" she cried, slamming her balled fist down on the armrest. "It was so close, and yet it failed!"

"It was *almost* enough," Helaine argued. "A little more power and it would have worked."

"Then take me to Treen," Destiny begged. "You can surely cure me there."

Pixel's heart was almost broken by the hunger and despair in her voice. They had to help her, somehow. "We may not need to go to Treen," he told her. "The problem is that your strength isn't as much as Score's. If he were linked with us, I'm sure it would work."

"Then let's wake him up and try it," Destiny said.

"No." Pixel shook his head. "Once he's cured, *then* we can cure you. Right now, he has no strength to spare. So it's imperative that we find the locket fast. That way, we'll be able to cure both of you."

"I understand." Destiny smiled. "I'll do all I can to help you find it. In fact —"

She broke off as several people suddenly came into the room. Three of them were holding guns. The last man wasn't. He was tall, dark-haired, and dressed in an impeccable fawn-colored suit. He smiled at them without humor.

"Good afternoon," he said. "My name's Tony Caruso. And I've come for my son."

CHAPTER 7

Score's head felt fuzzy when he awoke, and it took him a moment to realize that he was looking up at his father from a wheelchair. It didn't make any sense to him, and he decided that he wasn't really awake. This was just a really bizarre dream. "Good grief," he muttered. "What a lousy nightmare."

"It's not a nightmare, Score," Helaine answered, her voice tense with anger and disgust. "I'm sorry. I should have known there was trouble, but I didn't sense anything."

"You tired your magic out attempting to cure Destiny," Pixel explained. "That's why you had no warning."

Toshiro stepped forward. "You will please leave immediately, Mr. Caruso," he said smoothly. "You were employed to find your son. As you can see, we have located him. Your services are no longer required."

Bad Tony whirled to glare at him. "Don't tell me where or when my services are required," he snarled, backhanding the businessman, sending him crashing into the closest computer terminal. "I do what I want to do, and nobody tells me no. Not the police, not my business associates, and certainly not you."

Destiny shot her father a venomous glare. "And you thought you could control him!"

Bad Tony gave her a cold, hard smile. "Kid, *nobody* controls me." He snapped his fingers, and one of his thugs stepped forward. Score recognized him as Brio, who had clearly recovered from the beating Helaine had given him. "Take my son to the car," Bad Tony ordered, glancing around the room. "If anyone pokes their nose out of this door for the next five minutes, it will be shot off their face. And anyone who doesn't think it'll happen had better have a real good burial plan."

Score tried to protest, but it was pointless. Brio grabbed hold of him and lifted him out of the wheelchair. Score caught a glimpse of Helaine's face and saw the fury in it. He knew she was planning to attack. But she didn't understand what that could lead to here on Earth. "Don't," he told her, his voice weak and broken. "He means it. He'll kill you."

"Listen to my son," Bad Tony advised her. "You've got a nice face, and my son obviously likes you. It would be a shame to put a hole between your eyes."

Score was carried by Brio from the room and through the house. It was hard for him to focus on what was happening, but he at least managed to keep his eyes open. He saw another gunman at the door, holding three of the staff at bay. Brio crossed to a dark limo parked by the side door, and then helped Score in. He wasn't too gentle about it, but Score was in no shape to complain. He was weaker than he'd ever been. He felt he was only hours away from death.

Why was his father doing this? What did he hope to gain by it? Was he so mad at Score that he wanted to hurt him even more than he had already? If so, he was too late. Score could hardly hurt more than he did now. It was hard for him to stay conscious, and even harder to make much sense out of what was happening.

The car filled with people, still holding guns. His father slid into the seat beside him, propping him up a little. At his barked order, the limo pulled away and flew down the driveway.

"We're heading back to the city, Matthew," Bad Tony said. "It looks like you're going to need a doctor, and I know one of the best."

"There's nothing a doctor can do for me," Score informed his father.

"There had better be," his father growled. "Or else there's going to be one dead doctor in town tonight. Now, quiet. Save your strength. We'll talk when we reach safety."

What was the use? Score accepted the inevitable and collapsed. In his delirium, he remembered his father, and all of the terrible things his father had done. He had prayed for most of his life to be free from this man, and now he was right back in his clutches. What a way to die!

The blurred, foggy memories abruptly stopped as he came awake again. He felt totally drained and completely helpless. He was in a bed in what looked like a very expensive hotel room. If this was where his father was staying, he was doing all right for himself. And probably squeezing the money for it from lots of poor victims. A doctor was checking Score's pulse, and shaking his head.

"Mr. Caruso, I don't know what's wrong with your son," the man said. "It's nothing I've ever seen before. It's not a virus, disease, or poison. It's as if something is simply interfering with his body, shutting it down."

"You got it in one, doc," Score said weakly. He remembered his father's threat from in the car, and turned to Bad Tony. "There's nothing he can do," he explained. "Don't blame him."

"You were always soft," his father growled. Then he nodded. "All right." To the doctor he added, "Get out, and take your bag of tricks with you." The doctor nodded, snatched up his little black bag, and fled. He obviously realized how close he had come to being killed.

Score studied his father, and discovered that for the first time in his life he wasn't afraid of the man. Score was so used to living with that numbing fear all of his life that he was astonished to discover it had nearly vanished. It took him a minute to figure out why that should be, and then he realized the answer.

First of all, Bad Tony wasn't *really* his father. Foster father, maybe. But Score wasn't his physical son. Score had discovered that he had been one of the Triad, the rulers of the Diadem, who had escaped being killed by being reborn as a baby on Earth. He had no real idea who his true parents were, since he knew nothing at all about his real, former life. That had been wiped out of his mind when he had been made into a child again. But — most importantly — it meant that Bad Tony had nothing to do with his creation. And, in turn, that Score wasn't contaminated by Bad Tony's genes. He had always been afraid that he would grow up to be like his father. The thought of that had scared him as much as Bad Tony himself.

Also, Score thought, he was dying anyway. There was nothing much that Bad Tony could do to him now.

Knowing this gave Score an odd kind of courage. For the first time in his life, his father didn't terrify him. No more than any other of the evil beings he'd faced.

Bad Tony turned to face Score again. "You're probably wondering why I spent so much time and effort looking for you, Matthew."

"Actually," Score answered, "I really don't care. I was mostly wondering why you're not in jail."

"Ah, that." His father — it was hard to think of him as anything else, despite knowing what he did — made a dismissive gesture. "I managed to escape. I'm number three on the FBI's most wanted list."

"Well, that must make you very proud," Score commented.

Bad Tony stared at him. "You've changed since I last saw you."

Score had to laugh at that. "In more ways than

you could dream. So have you." He gestured at the room, and then let his hand flop back down. He didn't have the strength to hold it up. "This is a bit classier than where you had me living."

Bad Tony shrugged. "A few of my plans matured while you were gone. Which leads me back to why I hunted you so hard. I've spent years building up my empire, Matthew. And getting arrested taught me a very important lesson."

"That crime doesn't pay?" suggested Score.

"Don't be ridiculous," his father snapped. "It taught me that my empire is only as strong as the people in charge. And right now, that's *me*." He leaned forward. "What I need is a second in command who I can trust." He grimaced. "You've met Brio. He couldn't even get you to come and see me without messing it up. That's the kind of people I have to deal with here. What I need is someone with brains and drive."

Score could hardly believe what he was hearing. "Let me get this straight. Are you trying to make me an offer I can't refuse?"

Bad Tony spread his hands. "Family is everything, Matthew. I want to train you to take this over in case anything happens to me."

Talk about unexpected! Score didn't know what

to say for a moment. Then he snorted. "Get real. *Family is everything?* This from the man who beat the daylights out of me every chance he got?"

"I did it for your sake," Bad Tony replied earnestly. "It was to make you strong."

"It didn't work," Score informed him. "It only made me hate you." He sighed. "Whatever gave you the idea it would do anything else?"

"My father did it to me," Bad Tony answered. "It made me tough. He laughed and loved me the day I first struck him back. It was training, and it did me no harm."

"No harm?" Score could hardly believe his ears. "You're in charge of a criminal organization, you're on the run from the FBI, I hate your guts, and you think that's *no harm*? What world are you living in?"

"There's always a downside to everything."

"A *downside*?" Score was astonished at his father's knack for missing the obvious — as usual. "There isn't an upside!"

"There's money," Bad Tony replied. "There's power. There's respect. And it can all be yours."

Score wished he could shake his head, but he knew he might faint if he tried. "I don't care about money. I can make as much as I like. Power doesn't interest me, because I've got more than you can ever dream of. As for respect . . . *that* I've got. You remember those two people with me, who you threatened? They're my friends. They'd lay down their lives to help me, and I'd do the same for them. *That's* respect."

Bad Tony shrugged. "If you like them, I'm sure we can find them a place in the organization, Matthew."

That made Score laugh. "Helaine would rip your hired goons apart the first time you tried," he said proudly. "She beat up three of them in thirty seconds flat earlier today. I'll bet you couldn't offer Brio enough money to face her without a gun in his hand. You've got a pack of losers here."

To Score's surprise, his father didn't get mad. "So, they're not the best," he agreed. "But we can get better. The two of us, together. We can do anything."

"You're not listening, are you?" Score was getting weak again. He'd have to sleep soon, but he knew it was important to get through to his father first. "There's no way I want to join you. And even if there was, it wouldn't matter. I'm *dying*. And there's nothing you and your contacts and your crooked friends can do about it."

"You *can't* be dying!" Bad Tony growled. "I won't allow it. Tell me how it's happened, and I'll fix it. I promise you."

Score was going to laugh at that, but then a thought managed to penetrate his fuzzy mind. "You know, maybe you can do *something*. You remember that locket my mother owned. The one with my baby hair in it?"

Bad Tony nodded. "She loved that locket. Yes, I remember it. Why?"

"That's what's killing me." Score found the energy to sit up a little straighter. "I have to get it back."

His father scowled. "I don't understand. What are you talking about? How can a locket kill you?"

"This may be hard to understand," Score told him. "But I have magical abilities. Power to do things that normal people can't."

Bad Tony shrugged. "Your mother was like that. She was a *strega*, a wise woman from the old country. She had the sight, and told me that greatness would come from you. That's why I began to train you early, knowing that you would take over for me."

"You got it all wrong, as usual," Score replied. He still had a little strength left, so it was important that he make his father understand. "Give me a dollar bill."

Bad Tony fished one from his pocket and handed it over. Score took it, and held the edges in both hands, in full view of his father. "Watch," he commanded. Concentrating the last of his strength, he focused on the bill. His special ability was to change things in small ways, and he concentrated as hard as he could.

The dollar bill shifted slightly, and became a twenty.

Bad Tony snatched it from his hands and stared at it. His eyes wide, he looked up. "You changed it!"

"I told you," Score explained. "I can do magic. If I were well, I could do a lot more. The problem is, magic can also harm me. Someone has that locket and is using it to hurt me. I have to find it soon, or I'll die. So — what did you do with it?"

"Magic," his father murmured, staring at the twenty dollar bill he now held. "This is fantastic. With you by my side, there will be nothing we can't do! You will make all things possible for me. Imagine, father and son together! We'll rule this town in weeks!"

"Will you listen to me for once?" Score yelled. The effort left him extremely weak. "I don't have weeks," he explained, as Bad Tony concentrated on him. "I have at most a few hours. If I don't get that amulet back, I'm *dead*. Do you understand me?"

"Sure, sure," Bad Tony said, patting his arm. "Don't worry. It'll be easy to get back. I know exactly where it is."

Score was astonished. "You do?"

His father shrugged. "Sure. I gave it to Toshiro when he asked for it. It didn't seem important at the time. I'll just send a couple of men to get it back. Just relax. It'll be here before you know it."

Score collapsed, his strength almost gone. Toshiro had the amulet all the time? But *why*? What was he up to?

And then another thought came to Score: Helaine and Pixel were with Toshiro. He must be planning on betraying them, too. They were probably being led into a trap.

And there was no way that he could possibly help them. . . .

CHAPTER 8

Helaine was furious, mostly with herself. How could she have allowed those men to take Score? So her magic had been drained by the attempt to cure Destiny, but that was no excuse! She was still uncertain just how effective those weapons called guns might be, but Pixel, Toshiro, and Destiny seemed to fear them. If they hadn't held her back, she'd have chased after Score and his father immediately.

"You'd just get yourself killed," Pixel told her angrily. "Those guns shoot small pieces of metal at very high speeds. They can make a nasty hole in your body before you get anywhere near the person firing."

Helaine made a sound of disgust. "That is no weapon for a warrior," she said scornfully. "It is the weapon of a coward."

"Yes," agreed Destiny. "But a *live* coward, as opposed to a *dead* warrior. Listen to Pixel; he is telling you the truth."

"So we just allow those men to walk off with Score?" Helaine demanded. "Destiny, he's *dying*. We have to do something."

"And so we shall," Toshiro replied. "I have failed here by not realizing that Mr. Caruso was so desperate to have his son back that he would defy me. I must make amends to you for this oversight, and set into motion a plan to recover him."

Pixel nodded. "If you hired him, then presumably you know where we might be able to find him."

Toshiro considered this. "Since he has defied me, I doubt he will be in the same place as before. But I will have my men check the place to be certain."

"He'd be an idiot to still be there," Destiny said bluntly. "And he wouldn't have been a successful criminal this long if he were a total fool."

Helaine was indignant. "If you knew he was a criminal, then why did you employ him?"

Toshiro sighed. "Because of his extensive contacts in the city. I knew his men would be able to locate Score when he arrived. I could not use the legitimate authorities because they would have asked too many questions that I could not answer. About magic, for example."

"And, also," Destiny added, "Score ran away from a foster home. The police have a record of him. If we had alerted them to his presence, they would have taken him back into protection. We couldn't afford that."

"Which is why I obtained his release from jail as speedily as I could," Toshiro explained. "If they had finished checking on him before I could get him out, he would have been in serious trouble."

"He *is* in serious trouble," Helaine pointed out angrily. "He's dying, and he's in the hands of his father. Score has told us that his father has mistreated him in the past. I imagine he may be trying to injure Score even now. So it is imperative that we recover him."

Destiny nodded. "And I've a couple of ideas how to do it," she said. "First of all, I did manage to track down a suite of rooms in a hotel overlooking Central Park that were booked under an alias Tony Caruso often uses. I suspect that this may be where he has taken Score."

Toshiro raised an eyebrow. "Very efficient," he said warmly. "I will see about arranging some men. We can raid the place and —"

"— get Score killed," Helaine said coldly. "No. He is our friend. We will recover him."

"You don't know New York," Destiny objected.

"No," agreed Helaine. "But we do know Score, and we do know how to handle trouble. Score did mention that there is a law against carrying weapons, but his father seems to be ignoring it, and I think it is time that I did, too. Can you help me with this?"

"Of course," Toshiro answered. "But you do not know how to use a gun, and it will take time to learn."

Helaine gave him a disdainful look. "I would not use a coward's weapon. I require something with a blade. And also a bow and arrow, if you have them."

"Indeed." Toshiro gestured to the door. "Please come with me."

"I'll stay here with Destiny," Pixel said. "I'm out of my depth with any weapons, but maybe I can help her with the computers, in case we can find out anything else."

Helaine nodded, and then followed the businessman to another room. This room contained what looked like a collection of art dedicated to his homeland. Helaine's eyes widened slightly at what she saw there. There were two complete suits of armor, made from wood by the look of things. And there was a wall filled with weapons of all kinds.

"Japanese fighting arts," Toshiro explained. "Decorative as well as functional. Do you know about throwing stars or nunchuks?"

"No," Helaine answered. "But I know about these." She picked up a short bow and a quiver of arrows. "They're perfect." Slinging them over her shoulder, she went on to where several swords were mounted on the wall. Unfortunately, the most superb swords were too large for concealment. There were several sets of smaller swords, though, in matched pairs.

"*Katana,*" Toshiro explained. "They are generally used together."

Helaine drew one of the slightly curved blades and then hefted it to get a feel for it. It was oddly balanced, but she could compensate. "I've never been very good with traditions," she said. "I'll take just this one." She returned it to its sheath. "This should work. I need a way to conceal my weapons . . ."

"I'm sure I can find something," he replied. "I will go inquire. I shall meet you back in my daughter's room."

Helaine nodded and headed back to Destiny and Pixel. Toshiro was being very helpful at last, now that his own plans seemed to have taken a turn for the worse. Helaine didn't have much of a plan of her own other than to locate and rescue Score. She'd work out the details later.

Pixel glanced up from the computer with a slight smile as she arrived. "We're getting somewhere," he announced. "I think we've figured out where the amulet must be hidden. There is, apparently, a very large building in New York called the Empire State Building."

"Score mentioned it," Helaine remembered.

"Yes." Pixel grinned. "It fits the clues we've been given so far. The picture clue was of the building. We saw it in fragments, but Destiny recognized it. The intersection of the thirty-four and the five must mean that it's on Thirty-fourth Street and Fifth Avenue. And the other clue was a map of Manhattan. It shows the place where we arrived, Central Park. And it says *where you start is where you end*. It has to mean that we should finish up here, of course. But first, the Empire State Building. I think that if I go there and use my ruby, I may be able to find the locket."

"Which is great news," Destiny enthused. "Once you've recovered that, you can use it to make Score well. Then the three of you can cure me."

Helaine realized with a little anger that Destiny was focused more on her own healing than on Score's safety. But then, she could hardly blame Destiny too much. She'd lived like this for years, and, besides, she didn't really know Score too well. Helaine shrugged. "Then we shall have to split up," she decided. "I will go after Score, while Pixel will go for the amulet. Once we have them both, we can link up and cure him."

"I wish I could go with you," Destiny said. "But I would only slow you down."

"We know you want to help," Pixel said kindly. "But you're right; there's nothing you can really do at the moment. We have to do this ourselves."

"Actually, there *is* something I can do," the young girl replied. "Neither of you knows New York at all, so you're bound to run into problems. I can at least offer you advice and assistance." She reached over to the computer desk, and pulled out two small devices that were clearly meant to be handheld. She gave one to each of them. "A cellular phone," Destiny explained. She showed Helaine how to open it up. "It's linked directly to me. You just press this button, and I'll answer. That way, if you run into trouble, I'll be able to help out."

Helaine nodded. That made sense. It was rather like the technological answer to telepathy, she supposed. "Thank you. Now, how can we get from here back to New York? I would prefer not to fly again, if that's at all possible." Her stomach rebelled at the mere thought.

"That's just as well," Destiny answered. "Bad Tony expected us to follow him. One of his men shot up the controls so we couldn't fly. A limo might get you back, but with the traffic problems, that could take a while. Your best bet would be the subway."

Helaine frowned. "What's a subway?"

"An underground train," Destiny answered. Then, obviously realizing that wasn't enough of an explanation, she added, "Carriages that are drawn by engines. They travel below the ground in tunnels and can move very fast."

"It sounds dreadful," Helaine said honestly. "But if it is fast, I will try it."

"Then you will need money," Destiny said. She opened a compartment in her wheelchair, and took out a stack of the green pieces of paper that Score had used earlier. "Take these; they will help."

"This is what you call money?" asked Helaine, studying the papers. They all looked alike, except that the numbers in the corner and the faces on some were different.

"Yes." Destiny explained about the different denominations, and Helaine began to understand the system. It was similar to on her own world, except there for trade they used coins of gold, silver, copper, and bronze.

"Do you use this *money*, too?" she asked Pixel.

"I don't think so," Pixel replied. "I believe it's all done electronically on my world."

Helaine didn't have a clue as to what that meant, but she didn't really care. "Then we are just about ready to go," she declared.

"You just need these," Destiny told her, handing each of them a sheet of paper. Helaine examined hers, and discovered that it was a map. It showed the hotel overlooking Central Park. Pixel's showed the way to the Empire State Building. "If you get lost or have any problems, call me and I'll help out."

At that moment Toshiro returned, carrying a long bag with handles. "This should be what you require," he said to Helaine. Indeed it was; her bow, arrows, and sword fit into it well. There was another of those tongue and teeth things on the side, which opened to reveal a pocket. She placed her phone, map, and half of the money in it. Pixel put his own into his pockets.

"Then we are ready," Helaine declared. "Where is this underground railway you mentioned located?"

"I will have the car take you to it," Toshiro told her.

"Once you are there," Destiny added, "take the subway to the city. Then change for another that will take you closer to where you need to be. You'll find it's a lot faster than walking." She gave them a timid smile. "Good luck, and stay in touch."

Helaine nodded curtly. Pixel thanked Destiny again for her help. He seemed to be quite taken with the girl. Helaine snorted to herself. Boys were like that; a pretty girl, and they were fawning all over her. Thank goodness Pixel never did that to her!

Then Toshiro led the way out of the house, to where another of the large cars called a limousine was waiting. He gave instructions to the driver and they were off.

"That guy has got to be rich," Pixel said. "I wonder how many more of these cars he's got?" He reached out and opened a small compartment to reveal a tiny food and drink area. "Wow! It's really stocked."

"It would be useful to have one of these on our journeys," Helaine said. "They move quickly, and carry their own food."

"But they run on gasoline," Pixel told her. "And there's not a lot of that to be found easily in the Diadem."

Helaine didn't know what he was talking about, but it was obviously a reason why they couldn't simply take a limousine with them when they left the Earth. A shame. She was actually starting to like this mode of transport.

The ride took about twenty minutes, and then the driver let them out. He gestured to a set of steps leading down into the ground. "You go down there and buy your tokens at the bottom," he explained. "Then follow the signs for New York."

Helaine thanked him, and started down the steps. It felt like the time they had gone into the goblin caves, though these caves were at least brightly lit. Quite a few other people were heading in the same direction, and Helaine had to take care that her bag wasn't jostled. As the driver had said, there was a booth at the end of the passage, where a woman sat taking the green paper money. Helaine handed over one of hers. "Two," she told the woman. The woman nodded, and handed her back some papers and small coins.

Helaine and Pixel stumbled forward, following the crowd. Their way was blocked by metal spikes that cut off the passageway. They wouldn't move, and Helaine didn't know what to do. Someone behind them called: "Move it, kid!" Helaine had no clue how.

An elderly woman tapped her on the hand. "You're from out of town, aren't you?" she asked, kindly. "Just drop a token in the slot. That coin, there."

Helaine did as she was told, and then discovered that the spikes rotated to allow her through. She thanked the woman, who smiled.

"I was new at this once, too. You going to the city? Then come with me. I'll show you the right way."

Gratefully, Helaine and Pixel followed her down another corridor, and then down a flight of steps. They were now in a vast cave that had been lined and lit well. Tunnels led off from it, with metal rails in them. Helaine started to move toward one of these, but the elderly woman stopped her.

"You have to wait on the platform," she explained. "Don't *ever* try to go down there. The rails are electrified."

That didn't make a lot of sense to Helaine. She had a vague idea of what electricity was, because lightning was made from it. She knew it was dangerous — she couldn't help wondering how the people of New York had managed to bottle up lightning, or even why they would want to do so.

A moment later, there was a howling sound, followed by a rattling noise. Helaine saw lights moving from one end of the tunnel, and then something that was obviously a train drew closer and stopped. She studied it curiously, and then jumped when two doors slid open without anyone touching them. This place was astonishing! If she didn't know better, she'd have assumed that this was being done by magic.

The elderly woman guided them on. The carriage was quite full, so Helaine had to grab hold of a strap. Then the doors closed, and the train started up with a shudder that almost knocked her from her feet. It shot through the tunnel, shaking and rattling all the while. It was probably the most uncomfortable form of transport Helaine had tried yet, but it did have one advantage: She couldn't see outside. It was totally black, which meant that she couldn't see how fast they were traveling. That suited her just fine.

The ride wasn't too long. As they came to another station, the elderly woman smiled and asked them where they were going. She then guided them to where they could take the trains they needed. Helaine and Pixel thanked her, and she went off smiling.

Helaine looked thoughtfully at Pixel. "Now we must part," she said. "Once you have the amulet, head for Central Park. I will do the same when I have Score. There is a small lake at the southern end. We will meet there."

Pixel nodded. "Good luck," he told her.

"Thank you. May fortune smile on you." Helaine turned and headed in the direction that the woman had told her to go. She knew which train she needed, and now she knew how this system operated. She would be at the hotel very shortly, and then she would work out how to save Score. It was that simple.

But, to be honest, she had to admit that she was also rather scared. She was coping, thanks to the kindness of others, but this was still a very strange town and one where she could easily run into trouble again. And added to that, she didn't know how long she had left to rescue Score. For all she knew, he might even be dead by now.

No! She would never think that. She *had* to be able to save him. It was impossible that after all they had been through, he would be dead now. She *had* to be in time.

She *had* to be!

CHAPTER 9

Pixel stood in front of the Empire State Building, looking up. It was actually quite impressive, at least for real life. He could see why it might be famous on this planet. But he wasn't here to be a tourist. It was important that he get on with his mission. He touched the ruby in his pocket, and focused in on the amulet.

This time, there was a much stronger impression. *Upward!* He had to be a lot closer. The clue had worked out after all. Now, how was he supposed to find the item? He walked into the lobby of the building and through the crowds. People were taking photos of the interior. Well, it was very nice, but he had no time for this. He had to get up. But how far? There was a man behind a desk, obviously some sort of a host. Pixel approached him and asked how he could get up.

"To the left," the man replied, gesturing. "Then right. Down a level, and you buy a ticket."

A ticket? Pixel was getting confused. Why did you need to buy a ticket to go up inside a building? These Earthlings were very odd. Still, he had no option. He followed the directions, and discovered that he was at some kind of an attraction. That at least explained the need for tickets. The line was fairly long, but it moved quickly. With the money that Destiny had given him, he bought his ticket for the "observation deck," whatever that might be, and then he followed the crowd to an elevator.

This at least he understood from his Virtual Reality. Elevators were devices to move you up to the next level of a game. Had he somehow become a part of a computer game? Or was this city just stranger than he had imagined? The ride up was swift, and he got out on the last level with the others. He had to transfer to another elevator, and then reached the observation deck.

It was astonishingly crowded. This was clearly a famous place in New York City. People speaking strange languages, most carrying cameras, swirled around him. He passed souvenir stands, many of them carrying items with large monkeys on them. He didn't know what that signified; perhaps a local god.

The view from the edge was quite spectacular. He could see all across this New York. There was a large area of green to the north that he realized was Central Park. He could see the river between New York and Long Island. There were many other tall buildings in view, which the visitors all seemed to appreciate.

But that wasn't why he was here. Ignoring the crowd, Pixel concentrated on the ruby again. His mind quested for the amulet, and he found it almost instantly. He could detect it just over the edge of the building. Pixel moved to the correct spot and looked down. The ruby showed it some six feet away, but nothing was visible.

It had to be under some kind of a spell, which made sense. There was no way without magic of some kind to hide anything under the gaze of all of these people. Using the ruby, he could see it lay on a netting that surrounded the building. Pixel didn't understand why there should be netting there, but that must have something to do with the Earthlings' way of thinking. It wasn't important. The problem was that with the wires and meshes around the building, he couldn't get to the amulet, even though he could "see" it with the ruby.

Now what? He had to recover it, or Score would die. But how? Aside from the ruby, he had three other gems that he could use to amplify his weak magical abilities. He had a beryl; that controlled the element of Air. But the amulet wasn't made of air. It was metal, which was controlled by the Earth gem. He had a topaz, which controlled Fire. Again, that wasn't of any use. And, finally, he had a jacinth. That would bring people or animals to him if he called them. It only worked on living things, though, so the amulet wouldn't come to him.

Pixel was in a jam. If only he had his full powers, he might be able to do something. If only he had Helaine's sapphire, which could levitate things! But weakened as he was, he was stuck. None of his gems seemed to offer him any help. Nothing he had could make him rise in the air.

Or could it? The beryl controlled the element of Air. . . . Pixel thought for a moment. If he couldn't get the amulet using Air, perhaps he could do it a bit more circuitously. He couldn't bring the amulet to him, but perhaps he could bring himself to the amulet. . . .

Holding the beryl tightly, Pixel concentrated. He visualized the air in front of him solidifying, making steps. He focused all of his remaining power into the task, ignoring the crowds who pressed about him. One of the tourists gave a cry and moved away from him, puzzled by something. Pixel raised a foot, and discovered that there was an invisible step in front of him. He had done it — he had made the air solidify! He moved to the next step, eager to be over and beyond the fence.

One of the tourists screamed, "He's going to jump!"

Pixel abruptly realized the point of the fence and nets. Some Earthlings must use this place to throw themselves to their death. He couldn't understand it himself, but he realized that it explained arrangements here. Still, since he wasn't trying to kill himself, he ignored the cry.

The security guards didn't. Three of them ran toward him as he reached the top of his invisible steps. The lead one called to him, "Don't be crazy, kid! Don't do it! Come down from there!"

Pixel smiled at him. "I'll be back in a minute," he promised. "I just have to get something."

"Don't!" the man cried, as Pixel stepped over the fence. He lunged for Pixel, but slammed into the invisible steps instead and fell, winded, to the ground. Several people screamed as Pixel moved down to the net. They clearly expected him to plunge to his death. They must think he was crazy. Pixel ignored them and hurried down his steps. The amulet was still not visible, but he could feel it when he reached for it.

Snatching it up, he walked back to the observation deck.

The crowd had fallen silent; several of them had fainted. Seeing a person walking on thin air must have been too much for them. Pixel felt rather guilty, but there was nothing he could do about it. He dissolved the steps behind him, so nobody else would be tempted to try what he had.

Chaos soon broke loose. Pixel probed the amulet, trying to break the invisibility spell. As he did, the three security guards leaped toward him. They must have been unhappy with his actions, Pixel guessed. They clearly wanted to take him into custody, which might mean the police again. Now that he had the amulet, Pixel couldn't risk it.

Using the topaz, he sent Fire at the three men.

All three flung themselves aside, trying to douse the magical flames without much success. Finally they ignored Pixel and ran into the building. Pixel released the flames, grinning to himself. He was doing very well. These New Yorkers were completely unused to magic, and he started to feel very secure. Slipping the amulet into his pocket, he hurried inside. The three guards were using some sort of fire extinguisher, which meant that they were too busy to pay attention to him. Great. He slipped into the elevator, and descended.

A few minutes later he was outside on Fifth Avenue. According to the map that Destiny had created for him, if he followed this road he would come to Central Park. He was feeling really good. So far his mission had gone very well. He had retrieved the locket and was on his way to the rendezvous with Helaine. Everything was fine.

He hurried along with the crowds, crossing the streets when he could until he came to the southern boundary of the park. He saw the horse-drawn carriages that Score had pointed out earlier, and the rows of trees beyond. Perfect! When the lights changed, he hurried across and went into the park.

Helaine had said to meet her by the lake at the south edge of the park. The path he was on led him there very quickly. He looked around, but there was no sign of her yet. He must have been a lot quicker with his part of the task than she had been. Touching the ruby, he focused in on finding her. In the tingling of magic, he sensed that she was still south of him. She must still be trying to get Score free. For a moment he considered going to try and help her, and then he realized that this wasn't a very good idea. Helaine was wonderful at fighting, and if he blundered in, he'd only distract her. The best thing was for him to wait here as they had planned.

But that was easy to say. He couldn't help wondering if she was in some sort of trouble. Maybe he really ought to go looking for her? Maybe she really needed his help. . . .

Pixel didn't know what to do. He agonized over the decision for several minutes before he realized that someone was approaching him. He broke out of his reverie and looked up.

It was Toshiro, hurrying toward him.

What was *he* doing here? It didn't make any sense to Pixel. "Mr. Toshiro!" he exclaimed. "Is something wrong?"

"No, my young friend," Toshiro replied. "Everything is perfectly fine. You have recovered the amulet?"

"Yes," Pixel answered. He drew it from his pocket. It was still invisible, covered by its spell, but he could feel the weight of it. "Why?"

"I needed to be certain," Toshiro answered. He turned back to call over his shoulder, "Destiny! He is here!"

Pixel turned to look. As he did so, he saw that Toshiro was moving toward him. He tried to turn back but he was too slow. The businessman reached him and clamped a damp pad over his mouth and nose. He took an involuntary breath.

Pixel found that his vision was getting all fuzzy and his legs no longer supported him. Buckling at the knees, he collapsed forward.

The last thing he heard was Toshiro saying, "Phase three is now complete. In moments, Score will be ours!"

CHAPTER 10

Score knew he was dying, and it left him almost with a feeling of peace. It wasn't so bad when he slept, because then the pain went away. And the dreams began.

Score couldn't remember his mother very well. She'd died when he was six, and the years after that had been sheer terror for him. That was when Bad Tony had taken to beating him. While he was awake, all Score could remember about his mother was that she had sung to him a lot, and comforted him. That they had huddled together to escape from Bad Tony. He knew she had long dark hair that shone in the sunlight, and big, dark eyes that seemed to see right inside you.

But when he slept, Score could see his mother perfectly. Oh, it was just dreaming, of course, and the things he dreamed probably never had happened and never could have happened. But they made him feel a lot better. If he died, then he would be with his mother again, and everything would be all right.

The only thing that made dying less attractive to him was that he had started to enjoy being with Helaine and Pixel. He'd miss the two of them. And crotchety old Thunder the unicorn, too. Even Oracle. And Shanara, because she was so nice and very, very pretty . . .

Pain racked his body. He could feel death creeping up on him, shutting down cells and portions of his body bit by precious bit. Each time he dozed off he wondered if he would ever wake up. He enjoyed walking in his dreams with his mother through flower-strewn meadows, and talking to her. When he awoke again, he couldn't remember what they had actually talked about, but he was left with a feeling of peace . . . until the first spasm of pain kicked in again.

Score drank some water, the only thing he could keep down. He hadn't eaten since he'd come to

Earth, however long ago that had been. He simply had no stomach for food. He glanced blearily at the clock beside the bed. It was 4:32, presumably in the afternoon. It had to be the same day he had arrived, because Score knew he'd never have survived a full night.

Why had he woken up? Even though he was tired, he couldn't settle back to sleep. Something was nagging at him, something that wouldn't allow him to dream.

Then it came again, and Score realized what was happening. *Score! Are you still with us?*

Helaine? he called back, forced to concentrate and knowing how weak his mental voice would be. *Where are you?*

I knew you weren't dead yet, she said in relief. *You're too argumentative to let Death take you without a fight. Hang on, I'm coming in after you.*

Hang on? Score was worried and shocked. *Helaine, my father's men will kill you!*

They'll try, she answered. *I'll be with you in a minute. I've got to go.* The mental contact was broken.

The idiot! What did she think she was doing? There were at least six or seven of Bad Tony's gang here in the suite of rooms, and they all had guns.

Helaine couldn't possibly take them all out. She was going to get herself killed!

Summoning every last ounce of his strength, Score knew that he couldn't just lie in bed and let her walk into her own death. He had to help somehow, no matter what the effort cost him. He couldn't let her die for him. Ignoring the pain as best he could, and fighting off the blackness that was trying to claim him, Score managed to stumble out of the bed. Leaning against the wall, he fought for his breath. His heart was pounding, and there was pain in every joint. He'd have to ignore it somehow. Using the wall for support, he staggered across the room to the door. Red slashes filled his vision, but he didn't care. Helaine (the idiot) would need his help.

It took him three attempts to grip the handle and open the door. He glanced through the gap, and saw that three of the thugs were sitting in the outer room. One was smoking, and two were playing cards. All three had guns close to their hands, and nasty looks in their eyes. They were here to guard him, of course, so he was safe from them. Helaine wouldn't be. And if there were three here, that meant that there had to be another three out in the corridor. How could Helaine get past them all?

Well, she was pretty resourceful. But she also

needed help. Score's fist closed over the amethyst in his pocket. This changed the size of anything he could concentrate on. He didn't have much strength, so he had to be careful. He concentrated on the smoker's gun first. He reached inside it with his power, and could feel the bullet in the chamber, ready to fire. Using the amethyst, he concentrated, and expanded the bullet very slightly in size. Now, if the man tried to use the gun, the bullet would jam, rendering it useless.

The effort left Score weak and trembling. He had so little strength left that he knew he wouldn't be able to repeat the magic on the other guns. Instead, he decided to try the jasper next. This gave him the power of sight, and took less out of him. He concentrated on finding Helaine. If he knew what she was doing, he might be able to help her somehow.

He found Helaine in the room above the gunmen's. She was approaching the window, and had made a rope out of shredded bedsheets that she had tied to the table in the room. In his fuzzy state, it took him a moment to realize what he was seeing. Then he smiled. Clever girl! She'd realized that there would be guards in the corridor outside the rooms he was being kept in, so she'd gone to the next floor up and somehow broken into the room directly above them. She was going to come down outside and then attack from there. She had a bow and arrow at the ready, and a sword of some kind strapped to her waist.

He was proud of her, but at the same time scared for her. She was still going to get herself killed. She'd be coming through the window in about thirty seconds. She might be able to get one of the thugs, but the other two were bound to shoot her. She just didn't understand what she was up against.

Well, he'd have to try and give her a chance. He released the jasper, and could now see the gunmen again. Score was on the verge of collapse, but he wouldn't let go until Helaine was safe. He gripped his chrysolite, which gave him control over the element of Water. The smoker was harmless now, but the two gamblers weren't. They were drinking beer from the bottle as they played. As one of them raised the bottle to drink from it, Score used all of his remaining strength on the liquid. He exploded it outward, heating it as he did so.

A trail of burning alcohol flamed over the man's face. He screamed and fell backward, flailing at his skin. Score's knees gave way and he collapsed to the floor, staring through the gap in the door. The man wouldn't be badly hurt, Score knew, and he was mostly suffering from shock. The other player, too, had jumped to his feet, and the smoker cursed and rose.

The window exploded, and Helaine was in the room. The bow was in her hands, and an arrow on its way before the men could react. Score grinned. She'd targeted the second card player, whose hand was fastest toward his gun. The arrow slammed into his shoulder, knocking him from his feet and into the wall.

The smoker's cigarette fell and his gun came up. It clicked harmlessly and he stared at it in shock. Helaine's second arrow sent him spinning to the carpet.

The other man had managed to beat out the flames on his face. Helaine used the hilt of her sword to stun him. Then she looked around the room and saw Score in the doorway, struggling to rise. She gave a cry and hurried to him.

"What do you think you're doing?" she demanded, helping him to rise.

"That's a trick question, right?" Score replied. "The correct answer is either *helping you* or *dying*."

"You idiot," Helaine told him. "But thank you for stopping that man with the gun."

"Anytime." Score was now too weak to stand

alone. His vision was also getting very shaky. "But how did you get in that room above this?"

"There was a maid with a key," Helaine said proudly. "I forced her to give it to me, and I locked her in another room, where she will be no trouble."

Score sighed. "Remind me to tell you all about telephones sometime," he said. "By now, I should think hotel security and the police are on their way, looking for a mad girl armed with a sword and bow and arrows. We'd better get out of here."

"That was my plan," Helaine answered. "Hopefully, by now Pixel has the amulet."

"Oh." Score tried to focus. "Then you guys figured out that Toshiro had it, and that he's behind this whole thing?"

"Toshiro?" Helaine stared at him. "You must be feverish."

"Oh, great," Score groaned. "You *didn't* know that. So I'm sure he's set up a trap, and Pixel's naive enough to walk right into it. And they're expecting us to do the same."

Helaine thought furiously. "But the amulet was hidden at the Empire State Building," she objected. "Why would he do that?"

"Figuring out plots is Pixel's specialty, not mine," Score answered. "Especially not when I'm in this state. But I'd say it was for one of three reasons, or maybe all three. First, to make me as weak as possible. Second, because if he kept it, we might have been able to detect it and figure out he was behind everything earlier. And third, I think he needed time to set up his *real* trap."

"Which is?"

"How should I know?" Score growled. "I'm dying. I can't think of everything. It's time you used your brain instead of your muscles for once. Incidentally, there are guards outside the door. How are we going to get out of here?"

"Well, first of all," Helaine replied, "I'm going to use my muscles." She scooped him up in her arms. "You're obviously not strong enough to walk, so I'll have to carry you."

"I always knew I'd get carried away one day," Score muttered. "I never figured it would be in your arms, though."

Helaine blushed, and glared at him. "I'm only doing this because we have no choice. Now, shut up and let me concentrate." She held her onyx in one fist, the stone that gave her the power to change her shape. Last time she'd used it, she'd become a unicorn.

"You don't have the power to shape-shift on Earth," he objected.

"I don't need to shape-shift," she replied. "I just

need something a lot simpler: an *illusion* of another form." She concentrated, and suddenly Score was being held in Bad Tony's arms. He was very impressed.

She opened the door, and stepped out. There were two guards in the corridor, both of whom looked at "Bad Tony" in shock.

"Boss!" one exclaimed. "How did you get back in here without us seeing you?"

Helaine managed to make her voice lower and raspy. It wasn't quite like Score's father's, but it would do. "There's been trouble, you idiots. Get inside and sort it out. I'm taking Score to safety."

Both men rushed into the room. Helaine stabbed at the elevator button, and the doors opened immediately. Once inside, she hit the button for the lobby. Score was still managing to stay awake, though barely. Helaine had obviously figured out how to use elevators, he realized.

"Not bad, eh?" she asked him, proud of herself.

"My father always calls me *Matthew*, not Score," he replied. "Even those bozos are going to figure it out sooner or later. Then they'll be on our trail again. But it was pretty good."

The doors opened, and Helaine carried Score out. He knew they were conspicuous, but there wasn't a lot he could do about it. He had no strength to stand up alone. He glanced across the lobby and said, "Trouble."

Helaine saw what he meant: Two police cars had pulled up outside the hotel, and policemen were getting out. As he'd feared, the maid must have called for help. "Now what?" she asked.

"You'd better stop looking like my father," Score told her. "He's a wanted man. You'll be safer as yourself." He glanced around. "Head for those chairs and set me down." There was a cluster of comfy chairs for the guests, which might be what they needed.

Helaine immediately became herself again, and she laid him gently in one chair, sitting herself in the one next to him. "They might be looking for me," she murmured as the police started to enter the lobby.

"Pretend to kiss me," he said. "That way, they won't see our faces."

"What?" Helaine looked outraged.

"Just do it," he gasped. "I haven't much strength left to fake that I'm enjoying it." She hesitated a moment, and then grabbed him clumsily, holding her face close to his. He could feel her breath on his cheek. "And tell me when the coast is clear," he added. "I can hardly see anything right now." He wished he were feeling stronger, so he could enjoy Helaine's discomfort more. She must be hating this, and he wasn't awake enough to appreciate her distress.

"They've all entered the elevator," she murmured.

"Time to go," he said faintly. "I'm sorry; I can't last any longer."

He closed his eyes and collapsed.

CHAPTER 11

Helaine stared at Score, afraid he'd died on her. But she was still close enough to him in their pretend-kiss to feel his faint breath on her skin. He wasn't dead yet, but he was very close. The time for subtlety was past. She scooped him up and hurried for the door. The doorman hastily opened it for her, staring.

"I guess my kiss was too much for him," Helaine told the man. She flashed him a smile, and hurried out.

Central Park was just across the road, but there was so much traffic! She had figured out by now that the best places to cross were by the strange lights that changed colors, so she dashed for the nearest one. She waited impatiently until it started to change, and then dashed across the road, heedless of whether or not the traffic had come to a complete halt. People were staring at her, but she no longer cared. All that mattered now was to get Score and the amulet together.

Then she plunged into the park. She'd memorized the map that Destiny had given her and she knew the way to the lake where Pixel should be waiting.

Except Score had said it would be a trap. That Toshiro had had the amulet all along, and plotted all of this. It didn't make any sense to Helaine, but she realized that Score was probably right. This meant that Toshiro had both Pixel and the amulet. And that he was laying down a trap for Helaine and Score.

Well, there was nothing she could do about that. If Toshiro had the amulet, then she'd have to allow herself to be captured in order to get it back. It was the only way to save Score right now. After that, she'd figure out some way to escape the trap.

Hopefully, this plan would work. If not, enough planning: She'd do whatever it took to save Score's life.

She arrived at the lake, and glanced around. There were plenty of people here, but no sign of Pixel. She sent a mental yell for him.

A second later, she heard his reply: *Helaine! It's a trap!*

I know, she answered. *Where are you?*

I've been taken up north, he replied. *Close to where we arrived. It's some kind of maintenance area.*

I'll be there as soon as I can. Do you have the amulet?

No. Toshiro took it from me. He's behind all of this, Helaine.

Score told me, she replied, hurrying from the lake and hoping she'd remembered the way back correctly. *Do you have any idea what this is all about?*

None, he answered. *And neither does Destiny.*

Destiny? she asked, surprised. She avoided a couple of cyclists and a man who had tiny wheels on his shoes.

She's here with me, Pixel explained. *She thinks her father's gone crazy. She thought he was just trying to get her cured, but she realizes it's more than that.*

He's not crazy, Helaine answered. *He's got something planned. I just wish I knew what it was. Look, I have to concentrate right now. I'll talk later.* She broke off contact.

Helaine was starting to weaken from all the effort. Score didn't feel too heavy, because he was so weak, probably. But the raid on the hotel room and carrying him around like this was draining her strength. She really needed to rest soon. But there was no time for that. She blocked out her fatigue and pain and concentrated on reaching the area of the park where they had arrived.

Her lungs were burning and her arms aching by the time she reached it. She sent out another call to Pixel, and got an immediate response.

Head east, he instructed. *On the path. There's a shed of some kind to the left. If you go in there, it has steps leading downward. We're in the tunnels under that. They must be for park maintenance or something.*

I don't care if they're for moles to have birthday parties in, she snapped back. *I'm coming in.*

The building was just where he'd told her, and it looked deserted. She knew that this couldn't be true. The door was locked, but so what? Helaine kicked out and slammed it open.

It was a little musty inside, and dark. She didn't need lights, because she saw the flight of steps leading downward. She paused only long enough to grab her sapphire from her pocket, and then plunged down the steps. At the bottom was a corridor leading further downward. She hurried through it, trusting that this was the right way. There were several doors that she passed, but she ignored them. Pixel was further ahead of her, and so, probably, was Toshiro.

The doors behind her opened, and she glanced over her shoulder. Several men stood dressed in the wooden armor she had seen in Toshiro's house. They were all armed with long, slightly curved swords. She was, of necessity, now unarmed herself. More men blocked her way forward; behind them stood Toshiro, a faint smile on his face.

"Checkmate," he murmured. It made no sense to Helaine, but she didn't care. "I have now captured all of the pieces I need. You will surrender yourself immediately."

"You will give me the amulet immediately," Helaine snapped. She placed Score down on the floor, propped against the wall. He was still unconscious, and still breathing — barely. "I don't have any time for games."

"You are in no position to bargain," he replied. He reached into his jacket pocket, and withdrew the amulet. Helaine gasped slightly, seeing what she so badly needed so close to her — guarded by four armored and armed men.

"I'm not bargaining," she snarled, furious at him. "I'm *taking*." She concentrated through her sapphire. This gave her the power of levitation. Not enough to make her fly, given her lack of magical strength on Earth. But more than enough to snatch the amulet from Toshiro's grasp and whip it through the air toward her. Toshiro gave a cry of anger. His men tried to grab the amulet as it flew past, but they were no match for Helaine's skill and grim anger. A second later, her fist closed around the locket, and she felt a surge of triumph. Quickly, she laced it around Score's neck.

She could feel the magical outburst as the spell draining Score's life was shattered. Its power to harm him was now broken. Helaine was exultant. He would recover — if they could make it out alive.

"Kill them," Toshiro ordered his men.

Helaine fell into a fighting stance as the first of the warriors moved in for the attack. He gave a cry, whirling his sword around. Helaine laughed, reaching out with the sapphire's power. She pulled the sword from the startled man's hands and into her own, just in time to use it to block the attack of the second warrior.

But there were eight of them, and she was tired. She wouldn't be able to hold them off for long. She blocked and parried another attack, but it came dangerously close to breaking her guard.

"Get them!" a familiar voice yelled from behind her.

She glanced back quickly and saw Bad Tony Caruso in the corridor with several of his men, including Brio. They all had guns drawn, and opened fire.

Helaine threw herself to the ground, trying to shield Score as best she could. This was the first time she'd actually seen many *guns* being used at once, and she was stunned at how efficient they were. As a bullet hit one of the warriors, he simply popped out of existence!

That meant trouble. If one of them hit her . . .

She saw Toshiro whirl around a bend in the corridor, seeking safety. Helaine looked up as Bad Tony strode toward her.

"What's going on here?" he demanded. "What are you doing with my son?"

"My friend," she snapped back, refusing to be intimidated by him. "Saving his life. What do you think you are doing?"

"The exact same thing," Bad Tony growled. His eyes widened as he saw the amulet around Score's neck. "You got it back!" He actually looked relieved. "Was Matthew telling the truth when he said that it would save his life?"

"Yes," she replied. "He's already looking stronger. But it will be a while before he fully recovers."

The gangster looked at her with fresh respect. "You saved my son. I owe you for that, and I always pay my debts. Right now, I have one to pay that stinking weasel Toshiro."

"So do I," Helaine informed him. "He's holding Pixel captive. His daughter is back there, as well."

"She's not his daughter," Bad Tony answered. "I did some checking up on him. He's never married, and there's no record of a daughter. There's no record of his past at all. If you ask me, he's lied to her, too."

"But why?" Helaine bent to pick up Score, but Bad Tony shook his head and gestured to Brio.

"He'll carry Matthew," the gangster said firmly. "You're a better fighter, and I'd sooner have you free to fight." He gave a shudder. "This game's getting beyond me. Why did those men vanish when we shot them?"

"That's not what usually happens with bullets?" Helaine asked.

"No." He gave her an odd look. "You really must be from way out of town."

"I'm from another world," she replied. Clutching her borrowed sword, she started down the corridor.

"If anyone else told me that," Bad Tony answered, following her, "I'd laugh in their face. Somehow, though, with you that seems about right."

Helaine peered around the bend, half expecting to be attacked. But there was nothing in sight. *Pixel,* she called, grabbing her agate. *I got the amulet for Score. He's going to be okay. But Toshiro's vanished on me. Where are you?*

Straight ahead, he replied immediately. *And he's here with us. He's got a whole army of these warriors of his down here. It looks like he's ready for trouble.*

Good, Helaine replied grimly. *Because he's going to get it.* She led the way, sword at the ready.

One of the men bringing up the rear of the party called forward, "The police are on their way."

"Great," muttered Bad Tony. "They must have followed us, like my men followed you. Things are going to get very complicated, very soon."

Which was all they needed right now. Still, there was nothing Helaine could do about that. It was weird enough that she was fighting on the same side as Score's father.

They reached the room where Pixel and Destiny were being held. The door was open. Inside, several dozen of the armed warriors were waiting for them.

"Get them!" Bad Tony yelled. He and Helaine dashed forward. Helaine saw Toshiro behind the warriors, but it wasn't possible to see either Pixel or Destiny.

Suddenly, she was fighting for her life. The first warrior whirled and attacked. She caught the blow on her own sword, twisted, and freed herself. She struck back, but he parried and whirled again. He was half-fighter, half-dancer.

Helaine was *all* rage. She struck again and then used the hilt of her sword in a backhanded thrust, slamming it into his skull with enough force to render him unconscious.

Instead, he vanished.

This caught Helaine off balance, causing her to stumble. The next warrior was ready to chop down at her when one of the guns went off, and the warrior popped out of existence. She looked back and saw that it was Bad Tony who had saved her life. "Thanks," she gasped, and then attacked again.

The crooks could finish off a soldier with one shot, but in these close quarters they might also hit their own men. So they had to take care. And if they allowed any of the soldiers to get too close, they were in trouble. One gangster screamed as he lost his arm to a swift blow. Helaine was concentrating on fighting the men who came at her but she could see vaguely that many of the warriors were evaporating, while only one or two of Bad Tony's men went down.

But it was still not good. There seemed to be an endless stream of warriors, and Bad Tony had brought only eight men. Two were dead already, and at this rate they would all be slaughtered before they managed to get through the army and free Pixel and Destiny.

Then there were new people in the fight, dressed in blue. Helaine realized that the police had caught up with them, and were now having to fight for their lives, too.

Helaine! Pixel's telepathic yell came. It caught her by surprise, and almost made her miss the thrust to finish her next opponent.

Later! she snarled back, as the next one attacked her. This time, his sword almost made it through her guard. It caught her arm, leaving a trail of red as she backhanded the man and then stabbed him. He vanished, and she straightened up for the next one. How long could she keep this up?

Now, he insisted. *These warriors aren't real.*

They are, trust me, she replied, blocking another blow. *They're really hurting people.* Another of the gangsters was down, dead.

They're some kind of projection, Pixel insisted. *Toshiro's creating them. As long as he's free, he can keep making more, until they overwhelm you. You have to stop Toshiro, not his soldiers.*

Helaine knew she could rely on Pixel's information. There was only one problem. *I can't get to him,* she called. *Figure something out.* He went silent, giving her time to finish off two more attackers.

It was getting pretty rough. She had two slight wounds and Bad Tony had blood on his neat suit. There were only two of his men and about six policemen left standing. They may have started out after Bad Tony, but they had realized that they had to fight alongside him to stay alive. She couldn't see Score anywhere.

Then the man in armor closest to her burst into flames, popping out of existence. So did the man behind him. Pixel was using his topaz, she realized. The wooden armor of the warriors burnt very easily.

Coupling Pixel's magical assault with her skill, Helaine forced her way through the attackers and rushed to where a shocked Toshiro was standing. With a happy smile, she halted her blade just as it touched his neck.

"Get rid of them," she ordered. "Or I get rid of you."

Toshiro looked into her eyes and saw that she would do precisely as she threatened. He swallowed, causing a trickle of blood to appear where the blade touched his skin. "Agreed," he gasped, terrified. She backed off slightly as he muttered something under his breath.

The rest of the warriors vanished immediately and the battle came to an abrupt halt.

With the weird army gone, Helaine could now see the room they were in. It was quite large, and almost empty. The policemen and crooks were standing by the entrance, many of them bleeding from cuts. There were several bodies on the floor. One of these was Score, who groaned and sat up. He looked a whole lot better than he had before.

Helaine was holding Toshiro near the center of the room. By the far wall, Destiny and Pixel were tied together, back-to-back, but unharmed.

"What is going on here?" asked one of the policemen.

"I was hoping to find out," Helaine answered. She gestured at Toshiro. "This man was behind that whole battle. He's also kidnapped my friend and, apparently, his own daughter. Well, whoever she is."

The policeman grabbed Toshiro, confused. "This is Mr. Toshiro," he said. "Head of one of the largest companies in the city."

"And a very dangerous man," Helaine added. "Hold him tightly." She crossed to where Pixel and Destiny were bound. "Hi again."

"Hi," Pixel said, looking very relieved to see her. "Are you going to cut us loose?"

Now that everything was over, Helaine was starting to relax. "Are you sure you want that?" she asked, mischievously. "You seem to like being close to Destiny."

"Stop clowning around," he insisted, blushing.

With a grin, she used the borrowed sword to slice their bonds. "Thanks for the help," she said. "Now, what's going on?"

"And what did you mean about him not being my father?" Destiny asked.

"That's what Bad Tony told me," Helaine explained. "It seems that there's no record of your birth."

Destiny looked astonished. She glared at Toshiro. "What does this all mean?"

"I think we'd all like some explanations," Bad Tony agreed.

"Definitely," added the police sergeant. He pointed his gun at Bad Tony. "And I'd like some cuffs on you and your men. You're all under arrest."

For a moment it looked like Bad Tony was going to argue, but then he let his gun fall to the floor. "Ah, what's the use?" He held out his wrists and the policeman handcuffed him. Two other policemen handcuffed Brio and the last gangster. "But can I at least hear what this was all about?"

The sergeant shrugged. "I guess you can." He turned to Toshiro. "Well?"

Score limped over to join them. Helaine couldn't help herself; she gave him a big hug. Then she blushed. "I'm glad you're okay," she told him, trying to regain her dignity.

"Me, too," he said. He ran a hand through his hair. "I'm still a bit weak, but I'm recovering now." He tucked the locket in his shirt. "And I think I'll wear this from now on, just in case."

"So," Destiny prompted. "What's this all about?"

Toshiro sighed. He seemed to be totally deflated. "Power, of course," he answered. "What else? I have money enough, but it cannot give me all that I desire. When I discovered that magic truly exists and works, I knew then that I would have to obtain it for myself. But I had no powers, which caused problems."

"Magic?" the sergeant scoffed. "Can you believe this guy?"

"Yes," everyone else chorused, which shut him up.

Toshiro continued. "I found a way to transfer power from a magician. To do that, I needed to drain the person almost to the point of death, using something that they owned. In this case, the locket. I was going to use it to drain Score's abilities into myself, so that I could become a true magician. But you surprised me by snatching the locket from me and restoring it to Score."

"And what about these warriors you conjured up?" Bad Tony demanded. "If you have no power, how did you do that?"

"Through Destiny," Toshiro admitted. "I sought out a child with magical abilities. I found Destiny shortly after she was born. She is very strong and I adopted her, raising her as my own. I used my methods to siphon off her abilities, and used them to make my army animate."

"It's all starting to make sense now," Score said.

"You seem to be getting better by the minute," Pixel commented.

"I'm feeling it," Score answered. "You guys saved my life — again. I'll never forget it." Then his eyes wrinkled and he grinned at Helaine. "I just wish I could remember that kiss you gave me."

"Kiss?" Pixel asked, clearly annoyed for some reason. "What kiss?" He glared at her.

Helaine blazed in embarrassment. "It wasn't a kiss!" she protested. "I faked it."

"Yeah, right," Score agreed, pretending not to believe her. Back from the brink of death for just a few minutes, and already he was teasing her! Well, she'd fix him! Later . . .

"I don't believe this wild yarn for a second," the police sergeant declared. "But it hardly matters." He slapped handcuffs onto Toshiro. "You're under arrest, too. I'll figure out the exact charges later, when I can make some sense out of all of this." He gestured to his men. "Take them away and read them their rights."

"A minute," Bad Tony begged. "Can I have a word with my son first?"

"Your son?" The sergeant was confused. "I guess, sure. No funny stuff, though."

"You've got my word on it," Bad Tony promised. The police backed off a short distance, but Score stayed where he was, beside Helaine, Pixel, and Destiny. His father looked embarrassed, and then said, "You're planning on leaving again, aren't you?"

"Yes," Score admitted. "There's nothing here for me."

"There's me," Bad Tony said simply.

"You?" Score shook his head. "You made me hate you and fear you for years. Well, the fear's all gone, but the hatred isn't yet. And you want me to stay so you can make me into another you. And I won't do it, ever. So yes, I'm leaving."

Bad Tony shrugged. "My offer's open, if you ever come back."

"Talk about an offer I *can* refuse," Score said. "Bye."

His father considered this, nodded, and then walked over to the police. They escorted him, Toshiro, and the two thugs out. The sergeant came back to the four youngsters. "You're going to have to come along, too," he said. "You're witnesses, and relatives, and God knows what else."

"Magicians," Destiny told him. She gave him a strong, hard look. "You don't need us," she told him. "We're all free to go."

"Right," he said, cheerfully. "I don't need the four of you. You're free to go." He gave them a grin, and followed his men out.

"Sometimes," Destiny said, "being a magic-user has its advantages, doesn't it?"

"I'll say," agreed Helaine. She was warming up to this other girl. "Now what?"

"Now we cure Destiny," said Score firmly. "I'm feeling a whole lot better, and we owe her, big time. Besides, it's the nice thing to do."

Helaine nodded. "Let's go up above, though. It's

too confining down here." She turned to Pixel. "You want to carry her alone, or shall we help?"

He had the grace to blush. "Maybe the two of us together?" he suggested. He seemed preoccupied with something, but she had no idea what. After all, everything was over, and they'd won again.

CHAPTER 12

Pixel knew he should be relieved that everything was over and Score was healed again. And in one way, he was. But there was something still buzzing about in his brain. Only he couldn't quite bring it into the open. Something he felt that he'd overlooked. Well, it couldn't be very important, and right now they had more urgent things to do.

He and Helaine helped Destiny back up the corridor and up into the park. They went to where the Portal could be opened and sat beneath the trees.

"Now that I'm well," Score said, sounding like his old self, "there are two things I want to do. First, cure Destiny."

"And second?" Destiny asked.

"Pizza!" he exclaimed. Pixel and Helaine couldn't help laughing at that. He'd been talking about New York food ever since they'd known him, and Pixel realized that they hadn't eaten any since they had arrived.

"Then we'd better get started," Helaine said. The three of them sat in a circle around Destiny, their hands joined. "Focus," she commanded.

Pixel obediently bent to the task. He could feel himself linking with his friends, the power starting to flow. Together they chanted: *Senoj ados oc*. Unlike the link with Destiny, there was no weakness this time. The magic grew, and Pixel concentrated on healing Destiny's legs.

He felt the shock of the magic growing and moving. It left him drained and weak. The power danced about the young girl, and seemed to be entering into every pore of her body.

She gave a cry of joy, obviously feeling the same thing. Hesitantly, she pushed at the ground, her legs below her. Slowly, she rose to her feet. Pixel and the other two jumped up, ready in case she needed them. She could still fall at any moment.

But she didn't. Carefully, she took a step, and then a second, and a third. With a whoop, she laughed. "I can walk!" she exclaimed happily. "You did it!"

"It was nothing," Score told her. "Well, actually, it was, but I'm glad we could help. You certainly helped us."

Destiny laughed again, and then whirled around, intoxicated with her ability to move freely at last.

"Yes," Pixel said slowly, as something finally clicked in his mind. "You certainly did help us. Helaine, where's the cellular phone that Destiny gave you?"

"Oh, I'm sorry!" Helaine exclaimed. "It's in that room at the hotel. I had to leave it there when I rescued Score."

"It's all right," Destiny answered. "We don't need it now." She grinned. "Time for pizza, right?"

"Definitely," Score agreed. "And then we can go back home again."

"Home?" Destiny asked. "Isn't this your home?"

"Not anymore," he replied firmly. "New York's great, but it's just one place in the Diadem. We've got a castle on Dondar. You should come and see it."

Destiny's eyes widened. "Could I?"

"You're a magic-user," Helaine replied. "Of course you can. All you have to do is go with us when we leave."

And that was the final bit of the puzzle! "No," Pixel said coldly.

"Huh?" Score stared at him. "Are you okay, pal? What's gotten into you?"

"We've been tricked," Pixel said firmly. "Toshiro wasn't behind all of this. *Destiny* was." The *she* was behind the *he*.

Helaine and Pixel stared at him in confusion. Destiny looked shocked, but he was convinced that was simply an act.

"What do you mean?" she asked, innocently.

"Toshiro didn't have any magical power," Pixel said. "And he couldn't siphon off yours, no matter what bag of tricks he had in his technology. Science and magic don't mix. *You* were controlling him all along. The cell phones made me realize that there was something odd. He couldn't possibly have followed me, and with no magic he couldn't locate me once I'd recovered the amulet. He needed *science* to do that. Like the cell phones. He could tap into their signals and know exactly where we were. That's how he grabbed me when I reached the park. But Helaine had left hers in the hotel, so he didn't know where she was."

Destiny frowned. "Well, it was his idea for me to give you the phones," she protested. "It didn't occur to me that he wanted to use them to track you."

"And the clues that Shanara sent us," Pixel added. "Now I understand them. They mean that our foe is a *girl*. And that means Destiny."

Score shook his head. "This is one really wild idea of yours," he commented. "Normally, I think you're on the ball, but this doesn't make any sense. Why would Destiny do all of this? I mean, she knew we'd cure her if we could. She didn't need to make such elaborate plans as you're suggesting."

"That's right," Destiny said reasonably. "I'm very grateful for what you've done. Why on earth should I want to trick you?"

"Why on earth *exactly*," Pixel said. "That's why. You're stuck here on Earth. You said several times that you were trapped. I assumed you meant trapped in your wheelchair by your legs. But that's not what you really meant. You meant you were trapped here on *Earth*." He knew he had it right now. To Helaine and Score, he added, "Don't you see? *That* is why she laid this plot. Not just to get cured, though that was part of it. It was to escape from Earth again."

"You're wrong, Pixel," Destiny said gently. "How can I make you see that?"

"Very simply," he said, with a smile. "Stay behind when we leave."

Destiny looked stunned. "But . . . I thought you all *wanted* me to come with you."

"We do," Score said, looking very confused. "Pixel, are you sure you're not overreacting here? Is there some other reason you don't want her along?"

"Are you *jealous* that I'll join the three of you?" Destiny asked, acting shocked. "That you'll have to share your power between four from now on?"

Helaine scowled. *"Power?"* she asked. "What are you talking about?"

Destiny was confused. "Well . . . Pixel said you live in a castle, and you're magic-users, so *obviously* you're in charge. . . ."

"What did I tell you?" Pixel said in satisfaction. "She's just another want-to-be dictator, trying to latch on to us as a way to get into it. You see, no matter how good a magic-user she is, there's no way to make a Portal from Earth. You need one from another world, like Treen, where the magic is stronger. She's been trying to make us think she's on our side, and just a poor victim, so that we'd take her with us. And then she'd be free to do whatever she wants in the Diadem."

With a cry of rage, Destiny jumped at him. He hadn't been expecting this, and he felt himself held by her. There was a knife at his throat, and suddenly he didn't feel quite so bright, after all. "You *idiot!*" she snarled into his ear. "If only you had just let it be, instead of having to act so clever."

Score and Helaine were facing Destiny now, worried looks on their faces. They couldn't be as worried as he felt, though! He was the one in trouble right now. The knife felt like it was ready to slice him open. He could feel the anger and frustration penned up in Destiny as if it were a solid thing.

"It's no use," Score said coldly. "Give it up, Destiny."

"No," she growled. "I'm not going to be defeated now. Not when I'm so close. You're going to open the Portal for me, so I can get off this stinking planet again!"

"What are you talking about?" he asked her, feeling the knife pressed against his throat the whole time. This was certainly not the way he'd imagined being held by her! "You were born here. You've never been off Earth."

"Idiot!" she repeated venomously. "You don't have a clue, do you? I'm like Score! He was sent here by the Triad, wasn't he? Forced to be born again on this forsaken planet, to grow up again. Only, unlike him, I remembered who I was before."

"Sent by the Triad?" Score asked, confused. He was obviously going to blurt out the truth — that the three of them *were* the Triad reborn — and Pixel had a sudden feeling that this would be a very bad idea.

"Score didn't know that," Pixel said hastily. "We never told him that. We didn't want him to ask too many questions." Pixel prayed that Helaine and Score got his unspoken message, and didn't contradict him.

Helaine nodded. "Thanks for causing even more trouble," she spat. *Terrific acting!* Pixel thought, relieved.

"But why did they do this to you, too?" he asked her.

"I worked for them," she said. "And they discovered that a wizard named Sarman was trying to kill them. They had to escape, so they worked out a plan to do that. They were going to transfer themselves and their powers into people on the Outer Worlds of the Diadem, where they could hide until they could strike back at Sarman. They needed to try out the method, to make sure it would work, so they used me as an experiment. They sent me here, to Earth. But it failed. I arrived as a baby, but with all of my memories intact. So as I grew up I planned on escaping back to the Diadem." She glared at Score. "They did the same to you, a second experiment. But in your case, they even wiped out your memory. It was all for their own selfish aims."

Boy, has she got it all wrong! Pixel thought. But it was no time to set her straight. She obviously hated the Triad for what they had done to her. If she knew that he, Score, and Helaine were the Triad reborn, who knew what she might do to them? "And the crippling?" he asked, working around the knife at his throat.

"An accident, I imagine," she replied.

"No," Helaine said clearly. "I could feel there was something odd about it. It was caused by magic, which means that the Triad did it to you."

"Another of their sick gestures, then," Destiny answered. "What difference does it make?"

"No," Pixel realized. "The Triad was cold and heartless. But they weren't evil as such. They wouldn't have crippled you without a good reason."

"You *know* the Triad?" Destiny demanded angrily. "Have they corrupted you, turned you to their side?"

"No," Score answered, perfectly honestly. "We destroyed them. They no longer rule. Nor does Sarman. He's finished, too."

"Then *you* are the rulers of the Diadem?" Destiny asked. "It's better than I had imagined."

"No," Helaine said. "Nobody rules the Diadem now. We gave up the power."

"Gave it up?" Destiny clearly couldn't believe this. "Then you're fools! You could have ruled *everything*."

"We don't want to rule everything," Score replied. "We just want some peace and quiet. And pepperoni pizza."

"So, what's the truth?" Pixel asked. "You did something to offend the Triad, didn't you? So they punished you by trapping you here, didn't they?"

"I just wanted to share their power!" Destiny cried. "With my strength, they could have defeated Sarman. But they refused, and ganged up on me to exile me!"

"Another loony dictator after power," Score said in disgust. "How many more of them are we going to run into?"

"It's no good," Helaine told her. "We won't take you with us when we go. You're stuck here on Earth. But at least you're no longer crippled. Be thankful for that."

"No!" Destiny screamed. "Open that Portal *now*! I'm not staying here any longer! I'm going to reclaim what is mine by right. If the three of you don't want to rule the Diadem, then I'll do it. Open the Portal or I'll kill Pixel here and now."

"You're bluffing," Score said, though he didn't sound absolutely convinced.

"No," she said coldly. "I'm not. If you won't set me free, then I'll kill all three of you. At least I'll have that much pleasure. You have ten seconds to open the Portal, or I slice his throat."

Pixel knew that she meant it; it was no bluff at all. She was desperate to be free and she'd kill him if she didn't get what she wanted. He started to speak, but the knife pressed tight against his throat. He squeaked, but said nothing.

"Okay," Score said. "You win. Let him go, and we'll open the Portal."

"No." Destiny laughed. "He goes with me. I'm not going to trust you to keep your word. Five seconds."

"Agreed," Helaine said hastily. "But I have to contact Shanara. She makes the Portal."

"Do it," agreed Destiny. Her grip was firm, but at least she hadn't increased the pressure.

Helaine concentrated and a moment later the black gash in the air that was the Portal appeared. Destiny laughed delightedly. "Back off," she commanded. Pixel could feel something odd happening, but he didn't have words for what was happening. She pushed him from behind. "Through the Portal," she commanded.

He had no choice. At her urging, he stepped into the Portal, the knife still at his throat.

The two of them vanished.

EPILOGUE

Score jumped at the Portal as Destiny and Pixel vanished together. "Come on!" he snarled. "Once we're through that, we'll have most of our powers back! We'll be able to take her out easily."

Helaine nodded, obviously having thought exactly the same thing. Score heard her behind him as he jumped through the gash in space, ready, he hoped, for anything.

Except what he saw.

Shanara was standing there in the clearing on Treen, staring at them in bewilderment. Blink was sleeping in her arms. There was no sign of either Destiny or Pixel.

"What's happened?" Shanara asked, confused. "Where's Pixel?"

"He didn't come through?" Score asked, just as confused. Helaine was staring around, equally at a loss. "With a knife at his throat and a girl behind the knife?"

"No." Shanara shook her head. "I received Helaine's message to open the Portal, and then you two came through it."

"I don't understand," Helaine said. "They *must* have come through."

"Unless . . ." Score looked worried. "Is there any way to change the destination of a Portal once it's up and running?" he asked Shanara.

"Theoretically," she said, still unsure. "You think Pixel might have done that? But he doesn't have the knowledge."

"Not Pixel," Helaine said, realizing what Score was getting at. "Destiny. She switched the opening point when she went through it, and then switched it back for us. She's gone somewhere else!"

"Can we find out where?" Score demanded urgently. "We've got to get Pixel back safely."

Shanara shook Blink. "Wake up, you lazy flea-hotel! There's work to be done."

"Ugh," Blink said, shuddering. "My least favorite combination of words: *wake up* and *work*."

"This is no time to be lazy," Shanara scolded him. "Help me focus on the Portal before it closes. We have to discover where it was diverted to." She held him tightly. Blink yelped, but concentrated. A moment later, Shanara released him, and he fell to the ground, muttering and grumbling. At the same instant, the Portal closed.

"Well?" demanded Score. "Did you find out where she went?"

"Yes," Shanara said. She looked very pale and worried. "She must be totally insane!"

"She probably is," agreed Helaine. "But where is she?"

"She crossed to Zarathan," Shanara answered. "The Forbidden World." She saw their blank expressions, and realized that they had no idea what she was talking about. "You've never heard of it, obviously. Few people speak of it, and with good reason. It is also known as the Nightmare World. It's very unlikely they'll ever get off that planet. No one ever returns from there."

"Nobody plus three," Score said firmly. "We're not going to give up on Pixel just yet. He saved my life, and I'm going after him."

Helaine gave him an odd look, one of respect. "Right," she agreed. "We'll conjure up another Portal to take us there, too."

Shanara shook her head. "You really have no idea how foolish that would be," she said. "You cannot go there, least of all now."

"Why not?" Score demanded. "Destiny went there."

"As I said, she must be insane." Shanara gave a cry of exasperation. "It's called the Nightmare World because *things* live there, things that can only exist in nightmares." She stared at them. "If you fall asleep there, they become real. And they will devour you. If you go through now, tired as you are, you are doomed."

Score stared at her, and then at Helaine. Both Pixel and Destiny had to be exhausted.

How long could either survive on Zarathan?

ABOUT THE AUTHOR

JOHN PEEL is the author of numerous best-selling novels for young adults, including installments in the Star Trek, Are You Afraid of the Dark?, and Where in the World Is Carmen Sandiego? series. He is also the author of many acclaimed novels of science fiction, horror, and suspense.

Mr. Peel currently lives on the outer rim of the Diadem, on the planet popularly known as Earth.